# The Busy Woman's Sewing Book

"A time-efficient and sensible overview of sewing basics...clear, well-labeled diagrams...a solid choice...suggested for most stitchery collections."
Booklist, American Library Association

"An excellent reference no busy woman should be without."
Linda Turner Jones, Sew News

"The perfect choice for the sewer who already has basic skills, but little time."
Midwest Book Review

"Fascinating hints...wonderful sewing techniques."
Creative Product News

"A book simply couldn't be more exact or instructive on the subjects the authors cover."
Small Press Book Review

This book is dedicated to the busy woman who took time from her schedule of rearing four children and managing a farm household to teach me the joy of sewing. Thank you, Mother, for your patience and continued encouragement.

N.Z.

To my mother, Roberta Patterson, with fond memories of stringing buttons at her feet while she sewed at the machine...of making T-shirts with my sister for our dolls...sewing prom dresses in high school...exchanging tips today on the phone...sharing our love of sewing.

R.L.F.

# The Busy Woman's Sewing Book

**Nancy Zieman with Robbie Fanning**

**Revised Edition**

**Nancy's Notions, Beaver Dam, WI**
**Open Chain Publishing, Menlo Park, CA**

Co-published in Menlo Park, CA, by Open Chain Publishing and in Beaver Dam, WI, by Nancy's Notions
Library of Congress Catalog Card Number 88-90512
ISBN 0-932086-02-0 hardbound
ISBN 0-932086-03-9 softbound

Revised edition designed by Martha Vercoutere
Illustrations by Pamela S. Poole
Typesetting by Tony Fanning
Photos reprinted by Larry Brazil
Cover photo by Skip Ellinger

Original edition artist Laure Noe
Editors, Bonnie Arndt, Nancy E. Brown, Phyllis Novak
Photographer, Bonnie Arndt
Original edition ©1984 Nancy's Notions Ltd.

## ACKNOWLEDGMENTS

Special thanks to Pfaff American Sales Corp.; Swiss Bernina, Inc.; June Tailor, Inc.; Pellon Corp.; Crown Textiles; Stacy Fabrics Corp.; Kathleen Hasson, Donna Fenske, and Phyllis Novak; and all the consumers and other resources who shared valuable information for this book.

# Table of Contents

# Foreword to the Revised Edition
## by Gail Brown

*Gail Brown is the author of* Creative Serging Illustrated, Sewing With Sergers, Sew a Beautiful Wedding, Sensational Silk, The Super Sweater Idea Book, *and the* Instant Interiors *home decorating series.*

*She edits two sewing newsletters, "Sewing Update" and "Serger Update", and writes often for such sewing publications as "Sew News," "McCall's Patterns" magazine, and "Needlecraft for Today."*

*Gail lives in Aberdeen, WA, with her husband John and her two children, Bett and Jack. She is working on a book about sewing knits.*

Like most seamsters, I frantically search for sewing time in a schedule jammed with family and work. After the premature birth of my second child, I nearly surrendered to a sewingless life. But *The Busy Woman's Sewing Book* has convinced me that I can find time to sew. Thankfully, Nancy's finding-time-to-sew tips, and those of her many fans, persuaded me to try, try again.

Leave it to Nancy, one of the busiest sewing celebrities around, to show me there is time to sew, and to sew better. I shouldn't be surprised. During the ten years I've known her, Nancy has amazed me with custom-sewn gifts. These were not made by her staff, but by Nancy; the gifts are justifiably cherished by a friend and business associate who marvels at her thoughtfulness and productivity.

Yet the gift from Nancy I use most is her inspiration: that despite the demands of jobs, spouses, kids and homes, you *can* pursue another love--sewing. And still be human. Her collaborator, Robbie Fanning, is a first-rate writer in the sewing field, a time-management expert, and not coincidentally, the co-author of *Get It All Done and Still Be Human*.

Give yourself the gift of time by reading just a few pages of this book. The down-to-earth approach to sewing really wearable clothes is so refreshing. Perhaps that's why, with hundreds of sewing books at my disposal, I continue to count on *The Busy Woman's Sewing Book*. The tried-and-true time-saving tips and techniques have made my sewing faster--and more fun.

Gail Brown
Aberdeen, WA

# A Letter from Nancy

*Dear Sewing Friend,*

*If you like to sew, finding time to sew between cooking, cleaning, child rearing and working (to name just a few), requires organization. In addition, you need to make the most of your sewing time, which may require you to update your sewing skills. This book is designed to give you an updated, contemporary approach to sewing. You will learn techniques that allow you to sew an efficient yet professional wardrobe. Efficiency, without losing the professional look, is my approach to sewing.*

*In my Nancy's Notions Sewing Catalog, I have added personalized notes, called "Notes From Nancy," next to products that I have found of special interest. In this book, I have also added these notes, giving you added insight into a technique or a hint that might help you sew with greater efficiency.*

*In addition, many other sewers have sent in their favorite time-saving hints. You will find some of these in here. I hope these hints inspire you as much as they have inspired me.*

*My hope in writing this book is that you will enjoy these sewing techniques and will be able to sew a professional-looking wardrobe in a minimum of time.*

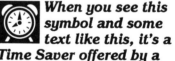 *When you see this symbol along with text like this, it's a* **Note From Nancy.**

*When you see this symbol and some text like this, it's a* **Time Saver** *offered by a fellow sewer.*

# CHAPTER 1

# FINDING TIME TO SEW

 *To organize my sewing time, I make a list of all items to be sewn and in which priority. I then group fabrics by similar color for these items. On one or two evenings, I pin and cut out and mark each item, placing each one in a large plastic Ziplock bag. In this bag also go fabric scraps, pattern, and any notions. These bags are then clipped on a multiple skirt hanger. Hanging them up takes less room, makes them visible, and enables you to know how much is left!*

*Irene Blakeley*
*Mission Viejo, CA*

In a day jam-packed with work, chores, duties, and appointments, how can we possibly find time to sew? In this book I'll show you the two major principles I use to save time for what I love: sewing.

The first principle is to save time by getting organized and I'll tell you more about my methods in Chapters 1 and 2.

The second principle is to save time by learning modern sewing techniques and using them over and over on basic garments. By perfecting one blazer pattern, one blouse and dress pattern, one skirt and slacks pattern, you can easily sew an entire season's wardrobe in a short amount of time. The rest of the book contains these techniques.

But I'm not the only one with time-saving ideas. Many other sewers have written to share their own tips. Some of them are printed here. I hope they inspire you as much as they've inspired me.

Here are the guidelines I follow in order to find time to sew:

### 1. Make a Plan.

First, decide *what* to sew. Then decide *when* to sew. If you have a clear idea of what you want to sew over the next few months, you will waste no time in indecision.

I like to plan a season at a time. With one good blazer, blouse, skirt, and slacks, I can go anywhere and feel well-dressed. Once I have these basic wardrobe items constructed, I can add extra blouses, sportswear, evening wear, or whatever else I'll need.

Take the time to write down your plan. You will find that it subconsciously motivates you to sew more and more. If you don't have a sewing notebook, feel free to write directly in this book (assuming you own it!).

Once you know what to sew, the next task is when to sew. If you're lucky, you may be able to free large blocks of time, which we all know is heavenly. But more likely, you'll have to squeeze in 15 minutes here and there. Still, some sewing tasks like cutting out and marking are more pleasant if they are done at one stretch. How to free two hours for sewing?

One technique that works for me is to pick one night a week and write on my calendar "Sew, 7-9 pm." Somehow, writing it down makes it official.

Another technique is to take ten minutes first thing in the morning to set up my work area. I lay out the tools, patterns, fabrics, and interfacings I'll need that night. Then I waste no time that night getting to work.

But my major approach is to chip away at every garment, sewing a little here, a little there, until it's finished. It helps if you have no pressing deadline for wearing the garment. Then you aren't tense as you sew and you don't make as many mistakes. (I admit, though, that like everybody, I've sewn late into the night to finish something for the next day.)

### 2. Limit Your Choices.

Fabric and patterns come in a dazzling array of choices--and that's the problem. You and I don't have unlimited time to sew. Do yourself a favor by perfecting a few classic patterns that fit you well. Then make them over and over, changing colors, fabrics, and designer details each season.

Likewise, limit the colors you sew. This helps save time in two ways. First, everything you make will match what's already in your closet. Secondly, you can wind extra bobbins of the major colors you use. You can also use the same thread set-up in your sewing machine and serger for more than one garment. For example, I like to make two slacks and two blouses at the same time.

### 3. Buy in Bulk.

Shopping for fabric takes more time than picking it out and paying for it. You have to get to the store and return home, which sometimes takes more time than shopping. Here's where the plan you made in step 1

 *Use patterns over and over again. Become so familiar with them that the garments cut from them go together much faster than if using new patterns. I have a McCall culotte pattern that has been modified innumerable ways (I even made a "skort"). I have used this pattern at least a dozen times and have lent it to friends. I stabilized it with iron-on interfacing. It also makes a great culotte-type slip.*

*Helen Schulke*
*Chapel Hill, NC*

*When I shop for a project, I always buy everything I need to complete it. Nothing is more aggravating to a sewer short on time than to find out at 10:30 pm that you can't go any further because you forgot to buy a zipper, interfacing, or whatever. I also keep a tablet and pencil handy to mark down miscellaneous items that I need to replace (marking pencils, etc.).*

*Joyce Perhac*
*Pittsburgh, PA*

 *I combine my avid sewing interests with needed exercise. While riding my exercycle, I read through a pattern, plan a project, read a new sewing magazine, or brush up on a procedure for my next garment. After I've ridden my 30 minutes, I'm refreshed and eager to get on with my sewing.*

*Kathy Miller*
*Endwell, NY*

saves you lots of time. Take your plan to the store. Then buy everything you need to make all the garments on your list, including patterns, fabric, interfacing, and notions.

I live an hour away from the big stores, so I am thankful for mail-order shopping. It saves me a lot of time to order by mail. At the end of the book is a list of some mail-order sewing companies and magazines.

### 4. Buy the Best You Can Afford.

Over the years, I've found that it doesn't pay to buy cheap sewing supplies, tools, or fabrics. You end up spending more time frustrated, ripping and repairing, and less time sewing. But a garment made with good fabric and thread on a well-made sewing machine will last years. And it will make you sing happily as you sew.

### 5. Organize Your Space.

Take the time to make sure your sewing area is comfortable, efficient, and well-lit. If possible, try to find a place where you can leave your machine set up all the time. This does not require a lot of space; even a cardtable in the corner is better than having to set up every time you sew. Watch your own habits. Do you prefer to have a clean area when you start? Or would you rather have the garment you're working on in full view? If something is keeping you from approaching your machine, try to figure out what it is--a pile of mail, someone's laundry, bad lighting, an uncomfortable chair? Take care of it right away. Your workspace must be inviting to you.

### 6. Grasp Every Opportunity to Sew.

Even if you only have time to wind bobbins and to thread your machine, you have made progress. Be content with sewing only one seam before you're interrupted. The important thing is that you've *started*, and that's the hardest part of sewing. You will find that once you start, you will be so eager to continue that you suddenly won't have any trouble finding time. Yes, that time may be in short spurts, but eventually you'll finish the garment.

### 7. Inspire Yourself.

We sewers are fortunate that so many talented people freely share their skills via lectures, classes, associations, magazines, newsletters, books, TV shows, and videos.

Sometimes I come home from work exhausted, thinking I'm too tired to sew tonight. I run a bath, pick up a sewing book to read, and all of a sudden I jump out of the bath, rejuvenated, inspired, and eager to sew.

Keep up-to-date on sewing and you, too, will inspire yourself. I've listed some of my favorite resources at the end of the book.

A word about mental blocks: You may run into a roadblock with your sewing-- a shawl collar won't turn properly, a garment doesn't fit after you've put hours into sewing it, a machine may be cranky. My advice is: don't suffer alone. Find a sewing friend to help you solve the problem. Ask at your local fabric store; check with local sewing teachers; write your county agent; ask your friends. Someone out there knows how to solve your problem, so that you can get back on track to what you love best: sewing.

 *I have a cheap dining room table that folds down to 30" x 9" when not in use, but opens to 30" x 60". A card table extends to hold cloth and a small TV stand holds patterns. I sew mostly religious habits for a small group here in Chicago and one in California. I also do craft work like pillows and pot holders for my parish Christmas bazaar.*

**George Whitman**
**Chicago, IL**

# CHAPTER 2
# SEWING SMART

 *Sewing is one of the fun facets of my life. While I'm alive, no one else can have my fun. But the work (housework, cleaning, etc.) will still be here long after I'm gone. So when I have that fun urge to sew, the "work" waits. Be selfish--take time to have fun and enjoy things you like to do. Life is very short.*

*Clara Fenstemacher*
*Nipomo, CA*

 *I have three children (6, 8, and 10), two boys and a girl. While I'm sewing, I let them help. I have a machine that embroiders figures and they like to decorate some of their own clothing. After their bedtime, I can sit in peace to do my hand sewing and embroidery.*

*Kathryn Dalecki*
*Elkton, MD*

Most of us learned to sew a long time ago. Nothing is wrong with the techniques we learned then, but a lot has changed in the sewing world in the last 20 years, so techniques have also changed. For example, fusible interfacings have revolutionized tailoring--and serger sewing has revolutionized everything else. These new methods save time yet still give you a professional looking result.

You may be so used to your old methods, however, that you are slow to incorporate the new techniques I'll show you in this book. Let me make some suggestions on how best to use this book.

### 1. Make a Notebook of Samples.

As you read through the book, you will discover many clever ideas. It may be some time, however, before you have time to make the garment discussed. So take the time to make a sample of the technique and put it into your sewing notebook. You don't need to make a full-sized sample--doll-sized is often big enough to teach you the concept. And sometimes you can make the sample with typing-weight paper, sewing on your machine as if it were fabric.

### 2. Use Wax Paper.

Ordinary wax paper from the grocery store is one of my all-time favorite sewing aids. Lay it over any pattern and try out alterations, new cutting lines, etc. By lightly touching it with a dry iron heated to Wool, you can fuse two lengths of wax paper together. This means you can try on an altered garment before you sew it: overlap the altered wax-paper patterns at the seams, fuse, clip curves, and slip on. If you don't like the look or you haven't altered enough, it's easy to make another wax-paper pattern.

There are two ways to trace onto wax paper. One is to draw with a felt- tipped pen. The other is to "draw" with a tracing wheel. If you choose the latter, put a layer of padding, such as a length of wool, under the original pattern. Otherwise the tracing wheel won't leave a mark.

### 3. Change Your Pattern Instructions.

Once you've purchased your basic blazer, blouse, dress, skirt, and slacks patterns, compare the pattern instructions to the new techniques you've learned. What changes do you want to make?

Go through the pattern and mark in red where you want to use my time-saving techniques. Either write the page number where I show you the technique or cross out the old technique and write in the new.

### 4. Keep Track of Your Accomplishments.

I regret that I have not kept track of what I've sewn over the years. It would give me so much added pleasure to have a record of all those garments and gifts.

I urge you to set up some sort of sewing record. Robbie uses a spiral-bound notebook, some use 3"x5" index cards, others use three-ring binders, and still others write on the patterns they use.

I've included a chart at the end of the book to help you keep track of the garments you make each season as a result of reading this book.

I've also included a chart of family measurements at the end of the book. Be sure you write in pencil and date each entry. It's amusing to see the changes in body measurements over the years.

I hope you will write in this book (assuming, again, that you own it), highlighting parts important to you, writing your questions in the margins, taking notes as you watch my shows and others', revising the mail-order lists as the years go by. That's what I do in my favorite books and it often feels as if I'm having a discussion with the author, which adds to my pleasure in sewing. I hope it adds to yours, too.

 *I've taken a tip from fabric stores. When I want to try a new pattern, I make out a 3x5 "model garment" card on it. It lists all the things I need to make the garment and I attach a fabric swatch to it, once I find what I like. That way, I know I have everything I need to make the outfit. It also helps to put a sketch on the back of the card.*

*When I can't sew and have some new patterns I haven't tried before, I enjoy reading the directions while traveling somewhere. Once I've made it in my head, it goes a lot faster and often you can adapt it to make it go even smoother.*

*Becky Feld*
*Aurora, CO*

# CHAPTER 3
# A BUSY WOMAN'S APPROACH TO SEWING BASICS

 *I suggest you set up a three-ring binder as a sewing notebook. Sew samples of the techniques new to you, label them with name of technique and book page number, and store them in your new sewing notebook.*

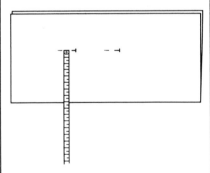

*Fig. 3-1* Grainline pins

When your sewing time is limited and you must make the most use of your available time, consider setting aside the traditional sewing techniques and updating them with a fresh approach. The best place to start is with the basics, techniques that will be referred to throughout this book and techniques that you will use in a multitude of sewing projects. These techniques will help make sewing time-affordable for your busy schedule.

## Shortcuts to Cutting

To easily cut out patterns that only have a few pieces (like slacks and tops), with a minimum of pinning and with a maximum of efficiency, try using fabric weights and "grainline" pins. Grainline pins are ordinary pins used to mark the grainline in fabric.

1. Pre-wash your fabric if you plan on washing your garment after it is sewn.

2. Fold the fabric right sides together, meeting the selvages.

3. Arrange the pattern pieces on the fabric to determine fabric layout. Measure the distance of the grainline of one piece from the fold. (If the selvage is uneven, measure from the fold. The unevenness is created by the tension put on the fabric during the knitting or weaving process.) Remove the pattern piece. Place a pin in the fabric at the measured amount. (This is a grainline pin.) See Fig. 3-1.

Place another grainline pin in the fabric 8-10" from the first. Place the pattern back on the fabric, matching the grainline of the pattern with the grainline pins. These grainline pins easily mark the grain of the fabric, without securing the pattern. This enables you to slide the pattern from left to right to economize on fabric (in other words, to save a bigger scrap to put in your scrap box). Repeat on all other pattern pieces. See Fig. 3-2.

4. Place pattern weights around the pattern. I use Weight Mates® or Shape Weights®, placing the weights at least 2" in from the cutting line. If the weights are too close to the cut edges, they inhibit cutting. Approximately four to five weights are needed. Place the weights on one piece. After cutting out the pattern, move the weights to the next piece. Grainline pins make pattern weights extremely workable.

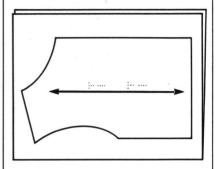

Fig. 3-2

## Marking

The most accurate and efficient pattern marking is a "nip," a 1/4" clip. You can easily substitute nips for cutting around notches and marking dots.

Instead of cutting around notches, cut them off at the cutting line and make a nip in the seam allowance. Dots can also be marked with nips at the adjacent seam allowances. See Fig. 3-3.

You can improve your marking efficiency with these notions:

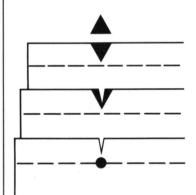

Fig. 3-3

- Washable marking pen: blue ink that disappears with a drop of cold water.

- Vanishing marking pen: purple ink that disappears after 24-48 hours.

- Ivory Soap chips: great for marking dark fabrics.

- Transparent tape: place a length of tape on the right side of the garment to make the topstitching lines. See Fig. 3-4.

## Fusible Interfacings

When your sewing time is limited, fusible interfacings are a must for almost every sewing project (rayon velvet being the main exception since the fiber cannot withstand the high temperatures or iron pressure). Fusibles add shape and stability with a minimum of effort. If you are not confident with fusibles, afraid that

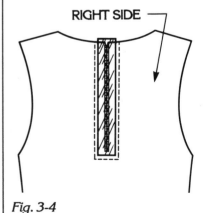

RIGHT SIDE

Fig. 3-4

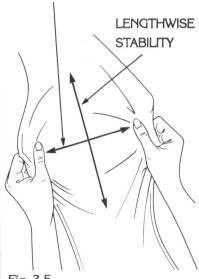

**Some instructions suggest pinking the edges with pinking shears to prevent the fusibles from leaving an imprint on the right side. If you must do this, the fusible is too heavy. Even the softest of corduroy can be properly fused without leaving a ridge if the correct weight is used.**

**If you cannot decide which fusible interfacing is best for your fabric, fuse scraps of fusible on scraps of your fashion fabric. I have found that fusing a circle is the best guide. It will be easy to see if an imprint forms on the right side.**

CROSSWISE STRETCH

LENGTHWISE STABILITY

*Fig. 3-5*

your fashion fabric will bubble, pucker, or become stiff, read these guidelines so you can make fusibles work for you.

### Guideline #1: Choose a Fusible One Weight Lighter Than the Fashion Fabric.

The adhesives on the interfacing which make it fusible add a hidden layer of weight. This weight is not noticed until the fabric is fused. To prevent the interfacing from leaving an imprint on the right side where the interfacing ends, *buy the interfacing one weight lighter than the fashion fabric.*

### Guideline #2: Put Like Fabrics Together.

There are five different base fabrics for fusibles: woven, non-woven, knit, weft-insertion, and hair canvas. Each base fabric will lend its characteristics to the fashion fabric, so the base of the fusible is another key to choosing the correct weight.

*Fusible Non-Woven*

From the newest non-woven fusibles for sheers to the more traditional non-woven fusibles like Stacy's Easy Shaper® and Pellon® Sof-Shape®, this category contains the greatest variety of fusibles. The traditional non-woven fusibles can be cut without a grainline, but necessitate a lightweight selection to prevent a change of the fashion fabric's hand. The more contemporary non-wovens with directional give in the crossgrain allow the fabrics to have the characteristics of knit or woven fusibles without stiffness. These must be cut on the grainline. See. Fig. 3-5.

*Fusible Woven*

This is a limited group of fusibles, but their choice should not be overlooked when sewing light to medium suiting weights. The blend of a woven fusible on a linen or linen-like fabric is a perfect match.

*Fusible Knit*

This category has only two entries to date: Stacy's Easy Knit® and Knit Shape™ Fusible From Pellon®.

The fusible knit adds shape and body to practically any knit fabric. It can also be used on wovens.

*Fusible Weft-Insertion*

The weft-inserted fusibles have a knitted base with a weft (crosswise) yarn inserted. Feeling almost like flannel, they are great for tailoring because they provide crosswise stability yet lengthwise stretch and recovery. Currently available in two weights, these fusibles are probably better known to you by their soft hand and trade names (Armo®-weft, Suit Shape®, and Whisper Weft®) than by the generic name "weft- insertions."

*Fusible Hair Canvas*

Like its cousin, sew-in hair canvas, fusible hair canvas is used for tailoring. This already crisp interfacing becomes crisper with the bonding agents. It should only be used with heavy woolens and wool blends.

### Guideline #3: Consider Color.

"Shade off" is the term used to describe what happens when the fusible causes the fashion fabric to change in shade. The new sheer fusibles are color coded and come in a unique range of colors (like red, blue, mocha brown, silver), to prevent the aggravating change of shade. See Fig. 3- 6.

### Guideline #4: Pre-treat the Fusible.

When the bonding agent is applied to the base fabric, the chemicals are applied at tremendously high temperatures. Most manufacturers feel that if the base fabric is going to shrink, it will shrink during manufacturing. The non-wovens do not need additional treatment, but for best results, *pre-shrink the woven, weft insertion and knitted fusibles*. Pre- washing eliminates the possibility of bubbling or puckering of the fabric. (Don't worry; it will not cause the bonding agents to "slough off" the base fabric.)

1. Submerge the fusible in lukewarm water, adding a small amount of dishwashing liquid to help the water emulsify. Let the fusible soak for 15 minutes.

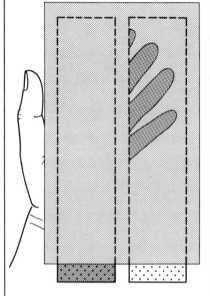

*Fig. 3-6* No shade off on the left.

Fig. 3-7

2. Rinse thoroughly and gently wring out the excess water.

3. Dry flat on a Turkish towel.

### Guideline #5: Cut the Interfacing to the Right Size.

Many of the cutting instructions require double work. First the interfacing is cut to the pattern size and then the seam allowances are trimmed off, a waste of both time and interfacing.

A simple technique using wax paper and a 6" sewing gauge can help make an interfacing pattern that is the correct size. The interfacing can be cut exactly to your specifications, with or without interfacing left in the seam allowances. I follow this general rule:

*Top-stitched Seam: Remove the 5/8" Seam Allowance.*

*Non-top-stitched Seam: Remove 1/2" of the Seam Allowance.*

This general rule allows all interfacings to be secured by machine stitching.

The illustrated collar will be top-stitched along the outer edges and along the neck edge. The interfacing is trimmed out of the top-stitched seams, but not out of the neckline seam. See Fig. 3-7.

Since an interfacing pattern piece is rarely included in the pattern envelope, make a new pattern out of wax paper. You will need wax paper, a 6" seam gauge, and a padded surface (a piece of wool works nicely).

1. Put the pattern piece on the padded surface. Then place a length of wax paper over the pattern piece.

2. Decide where you will topstitch on the garment piece and where you won't; then follow the general rule above. To leave 1/8" of fusible interfacing in the seam allowance, set the 6" seam gauge at 1/2". To remove all fusible

interfacing in the seam allowance, set the seam gauge at 5/8". See Fig. 3-8.

3. Working on the padded surface, guide the end point of the seam gauge around the cutting line of the pattern. Pay attention, because some pattern pieces, like the collar in Fig. 3-7, need two different settings of the seam gauge. The gauge will automatically make two lines on the wax paper: an outer line from the original cutting line on the pattern piece and an inner line.

4. Use the inner line on the wax paper as your cutting line for the fusible interfacing. Label the wax paper and store it for future use with your pattern.

### Guideline #6: Fuse in Place.

Fusing the interfacing takes time. Remember, patience is a virtue! Read the instructions that came with the interfacing, in case they differ from the instructions here. For example, your interfacing may require a damp press cloth. Be sure to test the interfacing on a small sample of your fabric, to guarantee that you will like the feel of the fused fabric.

1. Place interfacing, fusible side down, on the underside of the fashion fabric.

2. Cover with a lightweight press cloth or use an iron pressing plate like an Iron-All® or Iron Safe™ on the bottom of your iron.

3. With a steam iron set at Wool, press firmly for 10-12 seconds, counting "one thousand one, one thousand two," etc. Don't hurry!

4. Do not slide the iron to the next position. Pick it up and set it down. See Fig. 3-9.

5. If working with tightly woven synthetics like polyester gabardine, where the steam and heat penetration is difficult, repeat steps 1-4 on the other side of the fabric to ensure a good bond.

6. When fusing large areas, like a jacket front, spot fuse to keep the fusible from stretching. Fuse

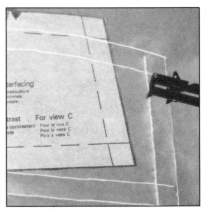

*Fig. 3-8* Use a seam gauge to make the new pattern.

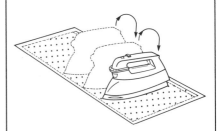

**At times, I've found that after the interfacing pattern piece is removed, it is difficult to remember which side of the interfacing is fusible. First I rub the interfacing on my cheek. The adhesive side feels rough. Then I mark the non-fusible side of the interfacing with a pin. This eliminates fusing the interfacing to the sole plate of the iron!**

*Fig. 3-9* Do not slide the iron.

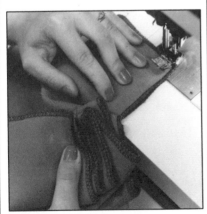

*The new presses, similar to the old mangles, exert about a hundred pounds per square inch on the working surface and are wonderful for fusing. You can fuse a number of garment pieces at once, all in 10 seconds.*

*I prefer to lock stitch rather than to back stitch. Back stitching often creates puckers that can be eliminated with lock stitching. Some of the computer machines have a button for an automatic lock stitch.*

*Fig. 3-10* Finger pinning

the top, bottom and middle to position the interfacing and then fill in the other areas.

### Seams

#### Sewing a Straight Seam Faster

We have all sewn seams using plenty of pins, but a long straight seam can be easily sewn with finger pinning, a ready-to-wear technique easily done at home. This technique is especially suitable for sewing straight vertical seams in skirts, slacks and dresses.

When sewing any vertical seam, remember the sewing principle of directional sewing. This means to sew the seam from the bottom to the top, sewing with the grain of the fabric.

Here's how to sew a straight, vertical seam using finger pinning:

1. Match the seam cut edges together. Place the fabric under the presser foot and lock stitch (sew two or three stitches with the stitch length set at 0). Remember to sew from bottom to top.

2. Match the raw edges at the top end of the seam; hold the fabric together with your right hand and pull the fabric taut. At the middle of the seam, pinch the raw edges together with your left hand and transfer to your right hand without letting go of the ends you already pinched. From the middle of the seam to the bottom (which is under the presser foot), match raw edges and pinch together at 6-8" intervals, always transferring the fabric to your right hand. Now you have four to five pleats or "finger pins" of fabric in your right hand. See Fig. 3-10.

3. Use your left fingers to hold the fabric layers together by placing fingers parallel to the seam, as if you were playing a flute. Sew to the first fabric pinch. Release a pleat of fabric and continue to sew. When you reach the second half of the seam, finger pin again.

The pinching of the fabric will prevent the fabric from shifting. Without finger pins, the top layer might end up longer than the bottom layer.

### Sewing an Eased Seam

To be efficient in your sewing means knowing all the capabilities of your machine. This is especially true when it comes to sewing layers together that are not the same length, such as the inseam of slacks, shoulder seams, and curved seams like princess styling in a jacket.

Whenever one edge is longer than the other, sew with the longer edge against the feed dogs. The job of the feed dogs is to bite or ease the lower layer of fabric, as the presser foot, with its smooth bottom surface, pushes the top layer of fabric. These two counter movements, the easing action of the feed dogs and the pushing action of the presser foot, cause the uneven lengths of fabric to meet. Therefore, *sew with the longer layer against the feed dogs. See Fig. 3-11.*

If you should sew from bottom to top, following the principle of directional sewing, and if you should sew with the longer layer against the feed dogs, following the principle of easing, what happens when you have a bodice like the one in Fig. 3-12?

The answer is that you will have to sew one of the complementary seams in an awkward position. If you don't, you will find one curved seam laying perfectly smooth, but the other side puckering. To prevent this, follow this procedure:

1. Sew one seam with the fabric laying to the left of the presser foot, the normal sewing position.

2. Sew the other seam with the bulk of the fabric to the right of the presser foot, between the needle and the head of the machine. It is slightly inconvenient, but well worth the extra effort since both seams will be sewn in the direction of the grain, with the feed dogs easing the uneven lengths. See Fig. 3-13.

Fig. 3-11

Fig. 3-12  Sew from bottom to top with the longest layer to the feed dogs.

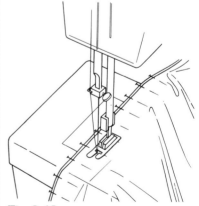

Fig. 3-13

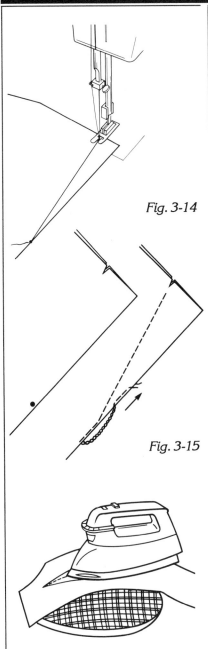

Fig. 3-14

Fig. 3-15

Fig. 3-16 Stop pressing 1/4' from the point so you don't make a bubble on the topside.

## Darts

### Sewing a Straight Dart

A straight dart can easily be sewn with a simple thread guideline.

1. Mark the dart legs with nips, 1/4" clips. Mark the dart point with a washable marking pencil or pen.

2. With right sides together, fold dart so nips meet. Place under presser foot and lower needle into fabric. Don't lower the presser foot yet.

3. Pull the top thread so that you have an 8-12" tail. Lower presser foot and lay thread on top of the fabric to mark the stitching line between nips and dart point. See Fig. 3-14.

4. Lock your threads by sewing several stitches at 0 stitches/inch. Lengthen the stitch to normal sewing and sew the dart, following the thread guideline.

5. At the dart end, turn the machine's handwheel, barely catching three to four stitches along the dart fold. This prevents a dimple.

6. Tie threads by chain stitching--i.e., sewing off the fabric, allowing threads to lock together. After chain stitching 1-2", attach the tail of stitches in the dart underlay. Sew two to three stitches in one place and cut thread ends. See Fig. 3-15.

### Pressing a Straight Dart

1. The first step in pressing any sewing is to press the stitching lines flat. This sets the stitches and makes it easier to press in the desired direction.

2. Since the purpose of a dart is to create a shape, press the dart over a shaped pressing tool like a dressmaker's ham. Press in the standard direction (vertical darts press to the center, horizontal darts press downward). Stop pressing 1/4" from the dart point. See Fig. 3-16.

If the fabric is bulky, cut the dart open, stopping 1/2" from the dart point. After pressing the dart flat, press the dart open. To avoid a dimple at the dart point, insert a metal tapestry needle to fill in the dart point and press over the needle. See Fig. 3-17.

3. Finish the dart by shape pressing from the topside. Be sure to use a press cloth or an iron sole plate like an Iron All ® or Iron Safe™ to prevent the fabric from becoming shiny.

## Finger Easing

When an area in a pattern needs to be eased (hem, sleeve, shoulder, etc.), we have traditionally been asked to sew two rows of basting threads, which are then drawn up by the bobbin thread.

You and me both have experienced the aggravation of these basting threads breaking when we're almost done gathering. This method of easing can also create too much of a gathered look, especially in a sleeve.

I like the machine method of finger easing, because it only requires one row of stitching and all of the work is done by the machine. This is a one-step method and does not require basting stitches. You will be surprised how accurately this eases almost every fabric. If you have not used finger easing before, practice on a fabric scrap to get the feel of the easing step. Set stitch length according to fabric weight: 8-10 stitches/inch for bulky fabrics; 10-12, for medium; and 12-14, for lightweight. Please test according to your fabric and your machine. See Fig. 3-18.

1. Sew 1/2" from the cut edge for sleeve or seam easing or sew 1/4" from the cut edge for hems. You will need only one row of stitches.

2. Press your finger against the back of the presser foot. Begin sewing, but try to stop the fabric from flowing behind the presser foot. Fabric will collect between the presser foot and your finger.

3. Sew 2-3", release your finger, and repeat. Although it is impossible to prevent the flow of fabric behind the presser foot, this finger easing

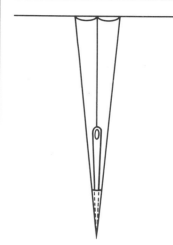

*Fig. 3-17*

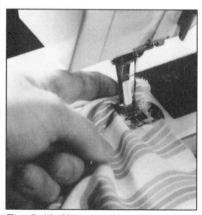

*Fig. 3-18* You can finger ease with either your right or left hand.

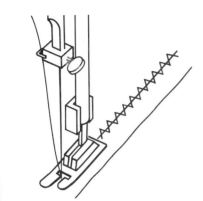

Fig. 3-21

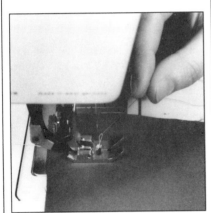

Fig. 3-19

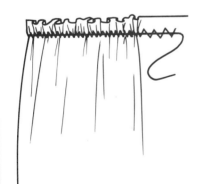

Fig. 3-22

causes the feed dogs to ease each stitch slightly.

This method gives the same results as the traditional method of easing, but in half the time. If you have eased too much, simply clip a stitch to reduce some of the tension; if you have not eased enough, pull a thread to gather more.

### The Busy Woman's Gathering Technique

The traditional method of gathering is to sew two rows of basting stitches 1/4" apart and then to pull the bobbin threads. While this method works, it's often difficult to distribute the gathers evenly, let alone keep the gathering threads from breaking.

The Busy Woman's Gathering Technique achieves even gathers by zigzagging over the bobbin thread. Here's how.

1. Take one stitch in the fabric. Bring the bobbin thread to the topside by gently pulling the top thread. The bobbin thread will appear as a loop coming through the fabric. See Fig. 3-19.

2. Pull the bobbin thread as long as the area to be gathered, along the stitching line. See Fig. 3-20.

3. Set the machine at a wide zigzag and a short stitch length (12- 14 stitches/inch or #1

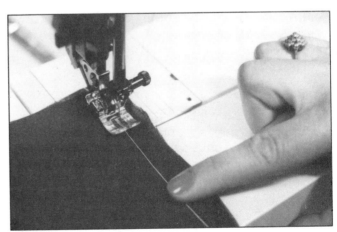

Fig. 3-20

setting). Sew over the bobbin thread. See. Fig. 3-21.

4. Gather by pulling the bobbin thread (Fig. 3-22). Since the thread is anchored in the first stitch, you do not need to worry about pulling out the gathering thread.

### Pressing

"Sew. Press. Sew. Press." I can still hear my mom repeating this phrase while she taught me to sew. When I was young, I got tired of hearing her say it; later I realized the importance of this basic sewing/pressing step.

Never join two seams together without pressing them, first flat and then open.

### Press Flat

On a cushioned ironing board, press the seam flat. This evens out the stitches and embeds them into the seam. Pressing the stitches flat now makes it much easier to press them open later. (Test it to see if it isn't true.) See Fig. 3-23.

### Press Open

After pressing the seam flat, press it open. Even if the seam allowances will be pressed in the same direction later, such as on a turned collar or a topstitched seam, follow this two-step procedure on all seams-- press flat and then press open. Later it will be easier to press the seam along its outer edge, giving you a sharp, professional look.

### Press Over a Sleeve Roll

To prevent the edges of the seam from making an imprint on the right side, press the seam over a sleeve roll. The rounded surface will press a flat seam without imprinting the seam edges on the right sides (See Fig. 3-24).

*If you do not have a sleeve roll, tightly roll a magazine or newspaper in a log shape and cover with fabric.*

*Fig. 3-23*

*Fig. 3-24*

Fig. 3-25

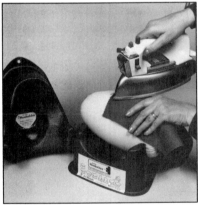

Fig. 3-26 Photo courtesy of June Tailor, Inc.

*It is extremely difficult to make your own pressing ham. If you do not have one, hint for one for Mother's Day or Christmas. Another gift idea is a Ham Holder. This tool enables you to use any shape of the ham while having your hands free to smooth and press.*

### Press a Serged Seam

A serger is a special machine that sews the seam, trims off the excess seam allowances, and overcasts the edges in one step. Depending upon the model, the serger may use three, four, or five threads to create the seam.

Follow this two-step pressing process to give a professional look to your serged seams. First press the seam flat, which evens out the stitches and produces a more even seam. Then press the seam in one direction (since the seam allowances are serged together, you obviously can't press them open). See Fig. 3-25.

### Press Curves with Curves

After sewing in a shape, such as a curve, keep that shape consistent by pressing over a like surface. Here is where having the right pressing equipment is as important as having the right sewing tools--and a *dressmaker ham* is essential, since many of the shapes and sizes we sew into clothes can be found on that uniquely shaped pressing tool. See Fig. 3-26.

### Stitching-in-the-Ditch

Hand sewing can be eliminated in many areas by stitching-in-the-ditch. This means to sew rightside up with a straight stitch in the valley created by the pressed open seam. The stitching will blend into the seam and will not be noticeable from the right side. On the wrong side, the stitching will catch the under piece. Use stitching-in-the-ditch on waistbands, cuffs and yokes to attach the back or facing side to the garment. See Fig. 3-27.

Fig. 3-27

## Understitching

Understitching means sewing the seam allowances to the under cuff, collar or facing. This stitching prevents these under pieces from rolling to the top side. Understitch any area to keep a facing from peeking out, even though your pattern guide may not mention this step.

To understitch:

1. Press the seam flat, then open.
2. Grade the seam allowances, trimming the seam next to the facing (undercollar or cuff) the smallest. See Fig. 3-28.
3. Press all seam allowances toward the under piece. See Fig. 3-29.
4. From the right side, sew the seam allowances to the under piece. To give even more support to the edge of the facing, collar or cuff, sew with a multi-zigzag or the widest zigzag instead of with a straight stitch (Fig.3-30).

Now that you've learned the basic techniques I use to sew quickly and professionally, let's apply them to the Busy Woman's Basic Wardrobe.

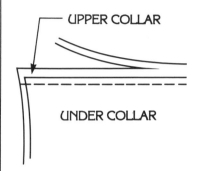

Fig. 3-28 Grading seam allowances

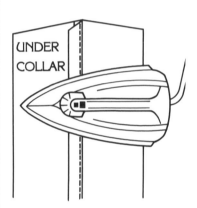

Fig. 3-29

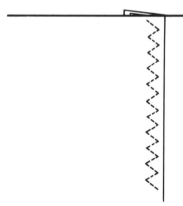

Fig. 3-30

 *I prefer to use a multi-zigzag for understitching. This stitch sews more thread per inch, creating a more tailored edge. I use this unconventional form of understitching on most woven fabrics and even on knits, to prevent the seam allowances from curling.*

# CHAPTER 4

# THE SEMI-LINED BLAZER:
# A CONTEMPORARY APPROACH

## THE BUSY WOMAN'S PATTERN CHANGES

Make your own sleeve heads and fusible shoulder pads, p. 34.

Wrapped corners on collars and lapels, p. 29

Extended facings for a professional look, p. 22

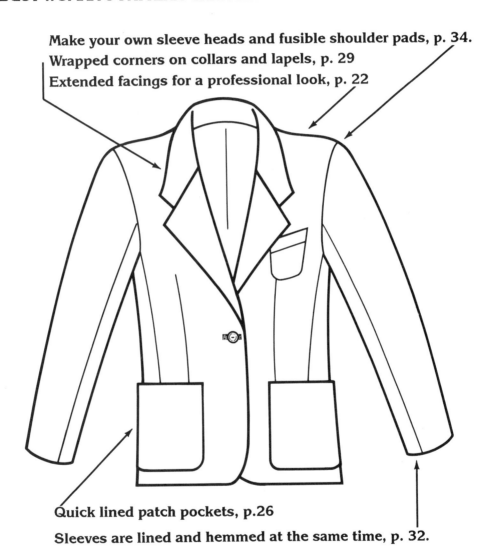

Quick lined patch pockets, p.26

Sleeves are lined and hemmed at the same time, p. 32.

A blazer is a mainstay in every wardrobe. In fact, I build each season's wardrobe around a blazer. In the past, we made them either lined or unlined. Lined blazers are comfortable to wear, hold their shape, and are fun to sew. But I do not always have the time to sew one. Unlined blazers take only a few hours to sew, but tend to lose their shape in the collar/shoulder areas. My unlined blazers looked more like loose fitting blouses and were difficult to wear, since the sleeves were not lined.

My solution is to build a season's wardrobe around a semi-lined blazer. It's the perfect blazer for the busy woman. It takes only a few hours to sew, yet looks like a lined blazer, holds its shape in the collar/shoulder areas, and is comfortable to wear.

Here's how, in only a few hours, you can sew a semi-lined blazer from your favorite lined or unlined blazer pattern.

## Purchase Changes

You will need to purchase different amounts of lining and interfacing for your semi-lined blazer than is given on the back of your pattern:

- **Interfacing:** 1 1/2 yards of 23-24" fusible interfacing (see Chapter 3 for suggested weights)
- **Lining:** 3/4 yard needed for the sleeves OR 1 1/4 yards if using heavy-weight wool or corduroy fashion fabric. In the latter case, the back facing will also be cut from the lining.

## Facing Changes

The facing pattern pieces on most lined and unlined blazers are shaped the same. The front and back pieces are both approximately 3" wide at the shoulder seam, with the front extending 4" wide down the center front.

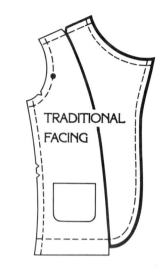

TRADITIONAL FACING

Fig. 4-1

*After you read this chapter and make samples, go through your pattern instructions and mark the areas you will sew differently.*

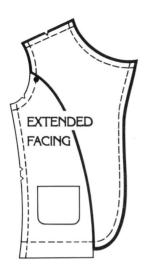

EXTENDED
FACING

TRADITIONAL
FACING

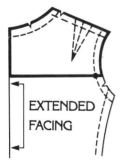

EXTENDED
FACING

Fig. 4-2

When wearing an unlined blazer with this facing design, the facings have a tendency to flip to the topside, which is annoying and unattractive.

Therefore, change the facing pattern pieces to extend into the seam allowances of the sleeve, giving greater shoulder shape while keeping the facings in place. You can also convert lined blazer patterns into a semi- lined blazer with these changes.

### Front Facing

1. Pin the front facing pattern to the jacket front pattern, matching notches. Place a length of wax or tissue paper over the pattern pieces.

2. With a felt-tipped pen, extend the facing's cutting line the entire length of the pattern's shoulder seam. Continue tracing the cutting line to the *center* of the armhole, where there is usually a dot in the stitching line. At the center of the armhole, gradually taper the cutting line back to the original facing. See Fig. 4-1.

### Back Facing

1. As you did with the front facing, pin the back facing pattern to the back jacket pattern. Cover the two patterns with wax or tissue paper.

2. With a felt-tipped pen, make the facing's shoulder seams the entire length of the jacket pattern's shoulder seam. Extend the facing to the center of the armhole, then across the back to the center back. If the pattern has a dart in the shoulder seam, draw the same dart in the back facing pattern. (When constructing the darts, press the facing dart in the opposite direction of the jacket dart.) See Fig. 4-2.

These extended facings will give your blazer more shape and support in the shoulder area. They will also hide the shoulder pads.

## Semi-lined Blazer Interfacing

A semi-lined blazer should be tailored, but with a softer look than the crispness of a custom-tailored blazer. This softer tailoring is achieved with the use of fusible interfacing.

Refer to Chapter 3 on choosing interfacing, making your own interfacing pattern pieces, and following fusing instructions. Remember this general rule:

***Top-stitched Seam: Remove the 5/8" seam allowance.***

***Non-top-stitched Seam: Remove 1/2" of the seam allowance.***

Following the general rule, the interfacing pattern pieces in Fig. 4-3 should have the seam allowances removed. At the same time, eliminate the interfacing from the back facing dart.

For shaping in the lapel, cut the interfacing 1/8"-1/4" from the marked roll line. Remove 1/2" of the remaining seam allowances. Add interfacing in the hem allowances, preferably cut on the bias, so when hemming, you can ease the extra fullness. Most patterns will not suggest interfacing in the hem of blazers, but adding it will give shape, body and stability. See Fig. 4-4.

## Seam and Facing Finishes

A semi-lined blazer requires seam and facing finishes to make the garment look as professionally finished on the inside as the outside. You can always zigzag the edges, but on ravelly fabric, thread whiskers can poke out. Try one of these methods instead:

***Consider using pre-cut fusible interfacing with a slotted row for the hem support. This product, Pellon® Fold-A-Band™, is used in ready-to-wear and is all-bias, so it will shape to the curve of your jacket hem. I find it speeds up my fusing time.***

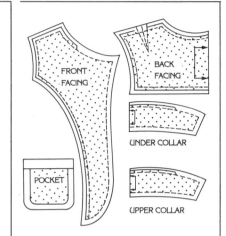

Fig. 4-3

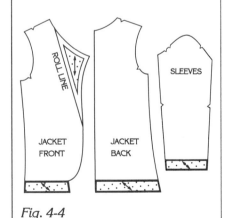

Fig. 4-4

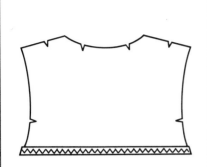

Fig. 4-5

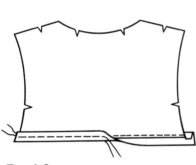

Fig. 4-6

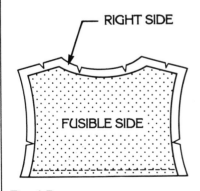

RIGHT SIDE

FUSIBLE SIDE

Fig. 4-7

## A. Finish With Seams Great®.

Seams Great® is a 5/8"-wide nylon fabric that neatly binds a raw edge without causing bulk. Since it is cut on the bias, it will mold around the curves of the outer edge of facings. See Fig. 4-5.

## B. Finish With Bias-cut Fabric.

Bias-cut fabric from your blouse/dress finishes the raw edges nicely and coordinates subtly with your outfit.

1. Cut 1"-wide bias strips of your blouse/dress fabric.
2. Rightsides together, place the strip on the facing or seam edge. Sew together with a 1/4" seam.
3. Fold bias strip around raw edge to underside of fabric.
4. Stitch-in-the-ditch, stitching in the groove of the seam to catch the underside of the strip. See Fig. 4-6.

## C. Finish With Fusible Interfacing (For Facings Only).

The technique of finishing with fusible interfacing takes a little more time, but gives an extremely neat look on jacket facings. The facing and fusible are sewn together along the outer edges. Then the fusible is pressed in place, creating a clean edge.

1. Cut fusible interfacing the finished size of the facing, minus the 5/8" seam allowances.
2. Rightsides together, sew facing and fusible together along the outer edge with an 1/8" seam. See Fig. 4-7. To sew easily around curved facings, shorten the stitch length to 12-15 stitches/inch.
3. Turn rightside out and finger press the sewn edge.

4. Fuse interfacing to facing. See Fig. 4-8.

### D. Serge the Raw Edge.

Finish the raw edge by using a two- or three-thread overedge stitch. To save time, chain the fabric pieces (Fig. 4-9).

### Lined Patch Pocket

Most unlined blazers do not have a lining piece for the pocket. Lining gives the pocket greater shape and will prevent the pocket from sagging. Best of all, this technique reduces the bulk that lining often creates. Sewing a lined patch pocket takes less than a half hour.

1. To cut the pocket lining, fold under the top hem allowance of the pattern and cut the lining from the resulting shape. Cut the lining on the *bias* to void excess raveling and for better shaping around the jacket contour. See Fig. 4-10.

2. Sew the lining to the fashion pocket along the hem allowance cut edge. Press flat to lining.

3. Before sewing, press the entire outer pocket to the finished size, using a piece of cardboard cut to the finished size of the pocket, a hem gauge, or a Pocket Former Template (see Fig. 4-11). If

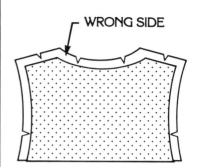

WRONG SIDE

*Fig. 4-8*

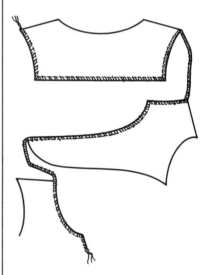

*Fig. 4-9* Chaining

**Save time when overedging raw edges by chaining the fabric pieces together. When all pieces have been overedged without pausing between them, clip the connecting chains. (See Fig. 4-9.)**

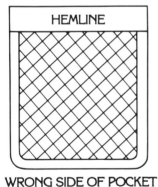

HEMLINE

WRONG SIDE OF POCKET

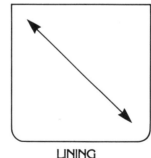

LINING

*Fig. 4-10*

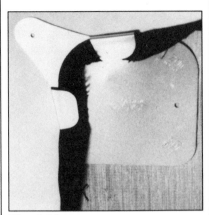

*Fig. 4-11*

***I am not a fan of notching bulk from corners; it tends to weaken the fabric and causes the corners to be uneven. But excess bulk can be eliminated by trimming the seam to 3/8".***

the fabric is bulky, trim the seam allowances around the corner to 3/8".

4. With rightsides together, place the pocket upside-down on the garment, matching the top of the pocket to the marking on the garment. Pin the lining over the pocket markings on the garment.
5. Mark 1" seam allowances on the lining. See Fig. 4-12.
6. Set your machine at a medium zigzag stitch. Start sewing at the pocket's top with a 5/8" seam and gradually increase the seam allowance to 1" by the time you reach the lining. Sew the lining on the 1" seam allowance. When you reach the hem allowance again, taper back to the 5/8" seam allowance, stopping at the pocket top. See Fig. 4-13.
7. Trim all the excess seam allowances from the lining only, trimming right next to the zigzag stitches. For close trimming, use applique scissors or bevel your scissors, cutting with the scissors flush or parallel with the fabric. See Fig. 4-13.

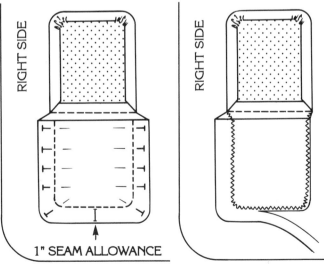

*Fig. 4-12*

*Fig. 4-13*

8. As a reinforcement, zigzag again over the first stitches.

9. Turn down the pressed outer pocket. Topstitch in place (or see topstitching alternative below). See Fig. 4-14.

Your lined pocket is complete. Since the lining has been sewn separately with a 1" seam allowance, the bulk from the lining has been removed, eliminating the possibility of the lining peeking around the edges.

### Topstitching Alternative

This technique is virtually invisible on wools, tweedy, or textured fabrics. Instead of topstitching the pocket, use a blind-hem foot and blind-hem stitch set at a medium width and length. Sew on the right side with the straight stitches in the ditch between the pocket and garment. The zig of the blind-hem stitch barely catches the pocket edge. See. Fig. 4- 15 and -16.

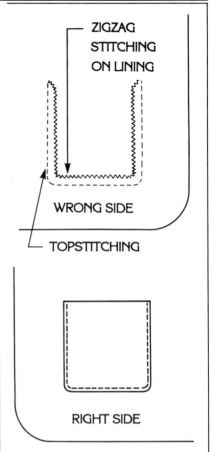

Fig. 4-14 Topside and underside of the pocket

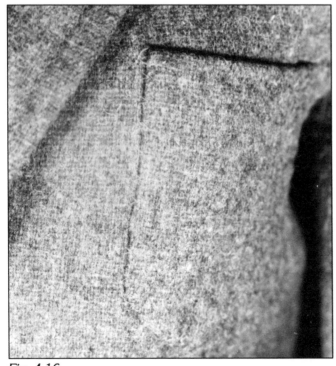

Fig. 4-16

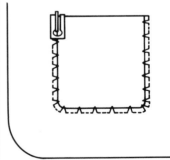

Fig. 4-15

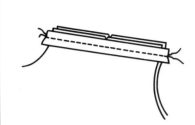

Fig. 4-17

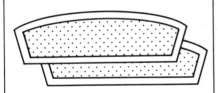

Fig. 4-18

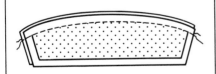

Fig. 4-19

## Shoulder Seam Stability

To add stability and to give the semi-lined blazer the custom-tailored look, add 1/4" *pre-shrunk* twill tape or Stay-Tape™ to the shoulder seam. Place a length of tape over the seam allowance and sew in place while stitching the standard 5/8" seam. See Fig. 4-17.

## Wrapped Corners on Collars and Lapels

When sewing a lined blazer, I use the usual four-point closure technique, a custom tailoring method. But when sewing a semi-lined blazer, I use a different time-saving method, the wrapped corner. It eliminates bulk from the collar and lapel, giving them both an extremely professional look.

### Collar

Your unlined blazer pattern may have separate pattern pieces for the upper and undercollar, or it may combine both into one piece. This terrific technique works on either pattern style. Remember that both upper and under collars have been interfaced. See Fig. 4-18.

1. Rightsides together, sew the collars together along the outer seam. Press the seam flat and then press open. See Fig. 4-19.

2. Grade the seam allowances with the undercollar trimmed to 1/4", the uppercollar trimmed to 3/8". See. Fig. 4-20.

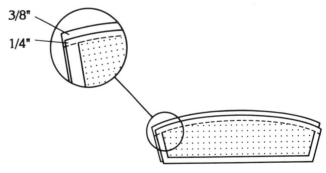

Fig. 4-20

3. Press seams toward the undercollar and understitch. See Fig. 4-21.

4. Sew the center front seam by folding the collar along the outer seam's stitching line. The seam allowances should be folded toward the undercollar. Start to sew at the fold and sew to the edge. Repeat on the other collar front--this is the wrapped corner. See Fig. 4-22. See my note below and Fig. 4-23 for a tip on smooth sewing starts.

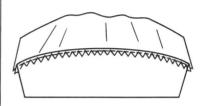

Fig. 4-21

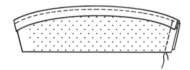

Fig. 4-22  A wrapped corner

 **Use multi-zigzagging when understitching a blazer collar. (See Chapter 3 for details.) This stitching sews more stitches/inch, creating a crisper, more tailored collar.**

 **Do you ever have problems with your thread knotting or your fabric being pulled into the feed dogs when you begin a line of stitching? If so, consider using what I have termed an anchor cloth. This is a folded scrap of fabric which I keep next to my machine. I sew a few stitches in my anchor cloth, butt the fabric up to the anchor cloth, and then proceed to sew.**

**My beginning stitches are even, my fabric has not bunched up or been pulled into the feed dogs, and my thread has not knotted. After the seam has been sewn, I simply snip the threads connecting the cloth to my seam. (See Fig. 4-23.)**

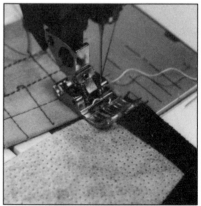

Fig. 4-23  Start with an anchor pad

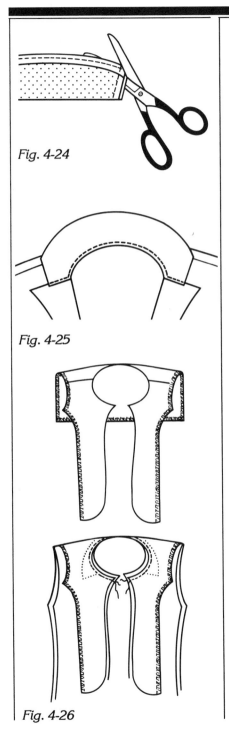

Fig. 4-24

Fig. 4-25

Fig. 4-26

5. Grade the seam allowances and angle cut the seams at each collar point. Press flat, then open. See Fig. 4-24.

6. Turn collar rightside out. Press.

7. Machine baste the collar to the neckline, using a 1/2" seam allowance. See Fig. 4-25.

## Lapel

8. After the front and back facings have been sewn together at the shoulder seams and the outer facing edges finished, pin the facing piece to the garment's neckline, rightsides together. See Fig. 4-26.

9. Sew the facing to the jacket neckline with a 5/8" seam allowance. Press the seam flat and then press open. Grade the seams, with the facing seam allowance being the smallest.

10. Press the seam allowance to the facing and understitch *only* between the shoulder seams of the back facing. See Fig. 4-27. Flip the facing back to the outside.

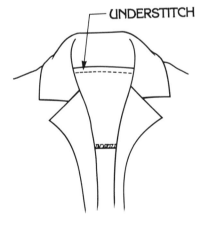

Fig. 4-27

11. At the lapel points, wrap the corner along the seamline, just as you did for the collar in step 4. The seam allowances should be folded toward the jacket side, not toward the facing side. Pin in place. See Figs. 4-28 and 4-29.

12. Pin the facing to the garment along the center edges. The facing is generally cut 1/4" longer than the jacket front, so that the facing will fit smoothly as it becomes the turned-back lapel.

13. Sew the front seam from the hemline to the lapel edge, jacket side up.

14. Press seams flat and then open. Grade and angle cut the bulk from the lapel point, as in Fig. 4-24.

15. Turn rightside out, using proper pressing techniques. This is one of the easiest and most professional collar/lapel techniques I know and is the perfect way to sew a semi-lined blazer.

## Lined Sleeve

One of the disadvantages of an unlined blazer is the unlined sleeve. A blouse or sweater tends to stick in the unlined jacket sleeve, making it difficult to slide on the jacket. That's why I add a lined sleeve to my semi-lined blazers. This technique doesn't take any more time than sewing it unlined, yet at the same time it gives the sleeve additional body and (my favorite part) automatically hems the sleeve.

1. Before lining your blazer sleeve, you must accurately determine the finished length of the sleeve. Place your hand on your hip. Have someone measure from the rounded bone at the end of your shoulder over the elbow to the wrist bone. With your arm bent, the right amount of ease is automatically built into the sleeve length. (Another way is to measure a

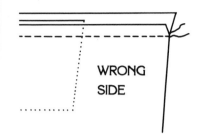

WRONG SIDE

*Fig. 4-28*

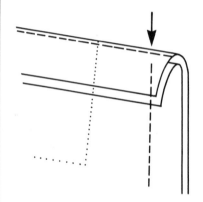

*Fig. 4-29* Wrapped corner on lapel

 **When ease stitching, always sew with the longer layer to the feed dogs. If you don't, the seam will pucker. Refer to Chapter 3 for greater detail.**

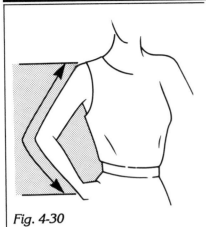

Fig. 4-30

blazer sleeve that fits you perfectly.) See Fig. 4-30.

2. Measure the pattern from the cap to the hemline. Alter if necessary. Fold under the hem allowance on the sleeve pattern and cut the lining from this pattern shape. See. Fig. 4-31.

3. Ease the fullness in each sleeve cap, both on the fashion fabric and the lining, using finger easing (see Chapter 3) between the notches.

4. Rightsides together, meet the raw edges of the hems. Sew with a 5/8" seam allowance. See Fig. 4-32.

5. Grade the seam allowance, grading the lining seam the smallest. Press the seam allowances toward the lining.

6. Rightsides together, match the underarm seams of the lining and fashion fabric and sew the entire underarm seam at once. See Fig. 4-33. Press the seam open.

7. Turn the sleeve rightside out and match the raw edges at the cap. Treat the sleeve and lining as one piece.

8. Set in the sleeve by matching the dot at the cap with the shoulder seam and by matching the two underarm seams. Do not force the notches

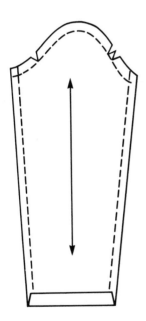

Fig. 4-31

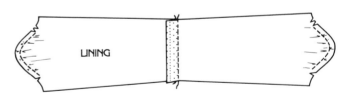

Fig. 4-32

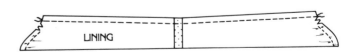

Fig. 4-33

to match. Stitch, then press the armhole seam flat.

## Sleeve Head

After the sleeve has been set in the jacket, insert a sleeve head. This is a small strip of fleece which helps fill out the fullness of the cap. If a sleeve head is not used, the sleeve may appear as if it is falling off the end of your shoulder.

1. For each sleeve, cut a strip of Needlepunch, polyester fleece, or Thermolam® Plus 1 1/2" x 10". (These materials are available in the interfacing section of your fabric store or through mail order.)

2. Trim the armhole underarm seam allowance to 3/8" and doublestitch. The cap of the sleeve should maintain a 5/8" seam allowance.

3. Meet the raw edges of the sleeve head to the raw edges of the sleeve's seam allowance, centering it at the shoulder seam. See Fig. 4-34.

4. Set the sleeve head in the sleeve by restitching the armhole from the garment side.

5. After the sleeve head is in place, work over a dressmaker's ham. Press the seam allowances and sleeve head toward the sleeve, pressing all layers in one direction. Be sure to press from the underside.

## Fusible Shoulder Pads

Always use shoulder pads in your blazers. They give that special finishing touch to the shoulder and sleeve area and make your blazer hang straight down from the shoulders, with no unflattering wrinkles.

You can purchase shoulder pads, but it's easy and economical to make your own. By tracing the shoulder shape of the front and back pattern pieces, you make a pair of shoulder pads that custom-fit the shape of the blazer.

*In Chapter 5, you'll find that the main purpose of notches is to tell which pattern pieces go together. Notches are not necessarily meant to match exactly.*

*In a sleeve, always match the dot at the cap with the shoulder seam and match the two underarm seams.*

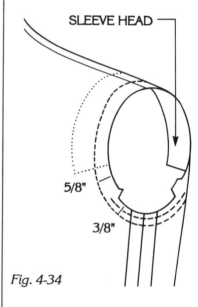

Fig. 4-34

*To avoid flattening the roll of the cap, always press the sleeve from the wrong side, never from the right side.*

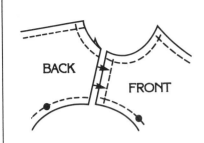

BACK

FRONT

*Fig. 4-35*

 *I lay three layers of wax paper over the garment and trace the shoulder pads. Then I can cut each paper smaller and still have a permanent pattern.*

**Sarah Bunje**
**Foster City, CA**

1. Fold under the seam allowance of the back pattern piece and pin it to the shoulder stitching line of the front pattern piece. See Fig. 4-35. Cover the shoulder area of the pattern with wax or tissue paper.

2. Draw the shoulder seam and the armhole cutting line between the center dots. See Fig. 4-36.(Since you already extended the facings to the center dots, the facings will eventually cover the shoulder pads.)

3. Place a pin at the armhole edge of the shoulder seam's cutting line. Tape string or thread to a felt-tipped pen and place the pen point at the front center dot. Anchor the other end of the string to the pin by winding it around several times. Draw an arc to the second dot.

4. Move the pen inward by 3/4", anchor the string to the pin, and draw a second arc, 3/4" smaller than the first. Repeat for the third arc. See Fig. 4-37.

5. Out of the largest arc, cut four layers of fusible interfacing. Out of the two smaller arcs, cut two layers each of polyester fleece. You now have

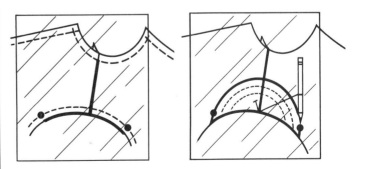

*Fig. 4-36*          *Fig. 4-37*

enough layers for a pair of shoulder pads. See Fig. 4-38.Make nips on all pads at the inner and outer shoulder seams.

6. Stand a pressing ham on its side and place one layer of fusible interfacing on it, *fusible side up.* Center the smallest arc of fleece on top of the fusible layers and then center the remaining arc of fleece over the smallest piece, matching nips. Complete the layers by sandwiching the fabrics together with a layer of fusible interfacing, *fusible side down.* See Fig. 4-39.

7. Place a few pins along the center of the shoulder pad and smooth the shoulder pad layers around the pressing ham. Since the shoulder pad is conforming around the ham, the lower layer of the interfacing will appear longer. Trim the interfacings so they are the same length (Fig. 4-40).

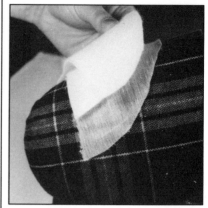

Fig. 4-39

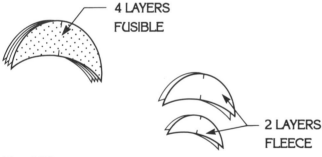

4 LAYERS
FUSIBLE

2 LAYERS
FLEECE

Fig. 4-38

**N N** *If thicker shoulder pads are required, simply cut additional layers of fleece. Depending upon the style, I've placed up to six layers of fleece per shoulder pad.*

Fig. 4-40

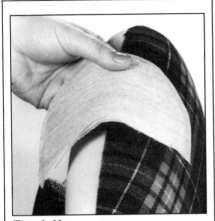

Fig. 4-41

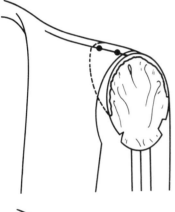

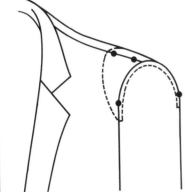

Fig. 4-42

8. With your steam iron set at Wool, fuse the layers together (Fig. 4-41).

9. Machine zigzag the layers together along the shoulder seam.

10. Place the shoulder pad in the garment, matching the raw edges of the pad to the raw edges of the shoulder seam allowance.

11. Tack the shoulder pad to the seam allowance at the cap, at the center armhole dots and at the neck edge. Always tack within the seam allowances, sewing shanks by hand (as with buttons) or by using your machine's fringe or tailor-tacking foot. (If this foot is not included with your machine, you can buy one.) Tacking the pads tightly without shanks may create dimples or pulls on the outside of your blazer. See Figs. 4-42 and 4-43.

When using the fringe or tailor-tacking foot, set the machine at the widest bar tack setting. As the thread sews over the high center bar of the foot, it will create a shank.

12. Finish the facing by attaching it at intervals to the sleeve seam allowance, using hand sewing tacks or machine sewing bar tacks.

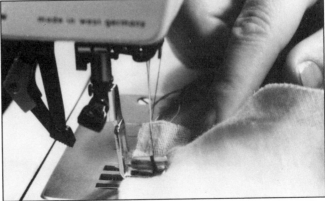

Fig. 4-43

## Finishing Touches

### *Buttonholes*

A corded buttonhole is a professional, yet quick buttonhole to sew on a blazer. The cording adds strength to the buttonhole and prevents it from stretching out of shape.

For the best thread match, the cording should be made by zigzagging over six strands of thread, using a stitch width of 4, stitch length of 1. See Fig. 4-44.

1. Loop the cording over the extra toe of your buttonhole foot. Some feet will have this toe in the front; others will have it in back.

2. Sew the buttonhole, sewing over the cording while holding the cording taut.

3. After the buttonhole is sewn, tightly pull the extra tails of the cording. This will slightly gather the buttonhole. Trim off the tails right next to the buttonhole. Now when you flatten and press the buttonhole, the cording ends will withdraw and be hidden in the stitches. See. Fig. 4-45.

### *Buttons*

Sewing on your buttons with your sewing machine, using the fringe or tailor-tacking foot, is a wonderful time-saving technique. The high center bar of the foot will create the buttons' shank. See Fig. 4-46.

Fig. 4-44

 *I cut labels out of my husband's shirts and sew them into my blazers: Calvin Klein, Dior, Gant, etc. Once someone said, "I didn't know Eddie Bauer made blazers."*

**Robbie**

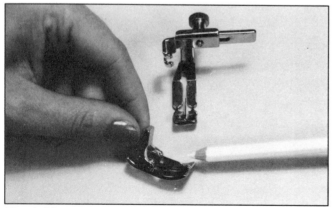

Fig. 4-46

Fig. 4-45

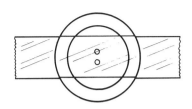

Fig. 4-47

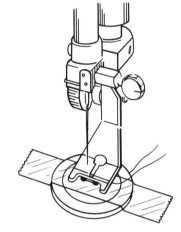

Fig. 4-48

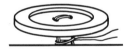

Fig. 4-49

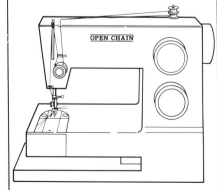

Fig. 4-50

1. With transparent tape, position your button on the garment (Fig. 4-47).

2. Set the machine at the left needle position, ready for bar tacking (0 stitch length, wide zigzag). Hand sew the first stitches, to check the correct width of zigzag for your buttons. See Fig. 4-48.

3. Zigzag five or six times. Lock the stitches by setting the stitch width to 0 and sewing several times in the left needle position. Cut your thread, leaving 10-12" thread tails.

4. When all the buttons are sewn, remove the transparent tape. Pull the buttons up, so that the excess thread forming a shank is between the button and the fabric.

5. Pull the long thread tails to the shank and wrap the thread around, as when sewing by hand. Tie the thread and lock it with Fray Check™, a colorless solution used to reinforce threads. It's completely washable and dry cleanable. See Fig. 4-49.

### Topstitching

Here are some time-saving hints for a professional look to topstitching.

### A. Use Double Threads in Both Top and Bobbin.

The conventional advice is to use buttonhole twist for topstitching. In my opinion, buttonhole twist doesn't have *enough* twist and tends to fray. I prefer to use double threads in both top *and* bobbin. Using a double-thread thickness in both places gives a more balanced tension to your topstitching.

If your machine does not have two spool spindles, wind two bobbins and stack them on top of each other on the thread spindle. Thread them through the guides as if they were one thread. See Fig. 4-50. Use double threads in the bobbin, too. Wind the thread for the bobbin with two threads at the same time.

## B. Use a Topstitching Needle.

These needles are size 14(90), with an extra large eye to accommodate two threads (Fig. 4-51).

## C. Sew With the Needle in the Left Needle Position.

In this position, the scarf (the groove in the needle) is closer to the bobbin hook and a completed stitch is more likely, with no skips. This is especially important since double threads are used on bobbin and top, which increases the chance of the bobbin hook missing the top loop.

## D. Sew a Step at the Lapel Point.

Make three pivots when you are topstitching the lapel point. Do not topstitch it with only one pivot. See Fig. 4-52.

1.  Place a pin parallel with the place where the collar joins the lapel (lapel point). Sew to the pin and stop. Pivot and sew to the lapel point.
2.  Pivot and sew two or three stitches in the collar seam.
3.  Pivot and continue to topstitch around the collar.

### Your Blazer is Finished!

Blind stitch the hem by machine and you're ready to wear your semi-lined blazer. The finished product should look as tailored as if you had spent hours of hand sewing--but all of it has been done at the sewing machine.

Now that the mainstay of your wardrobe is done, let's apply some time-saving techniques to blouses and dresses.

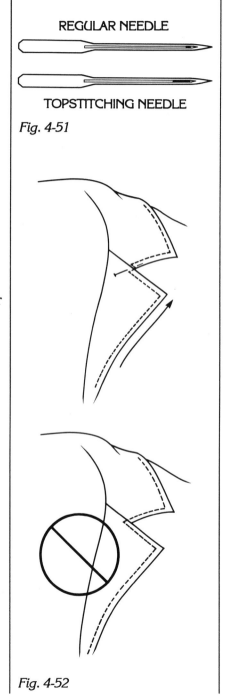

REGULAR NEEDLE

TOPSTITCHING NEEDLE

*Fig. 4-51*

*Fig. 4-52*

# CHAPTER 5

# TIME-SAVING BLOUSE AND DRESS TECHNIQUES

## THE BUSY WOMAN'S PATTERN CHANGES

Magic Collar, p. 47

Ready-to-wear front placket, p. 42

Serger sewing sequence, p. 62

Fast placket techniques, p. 52

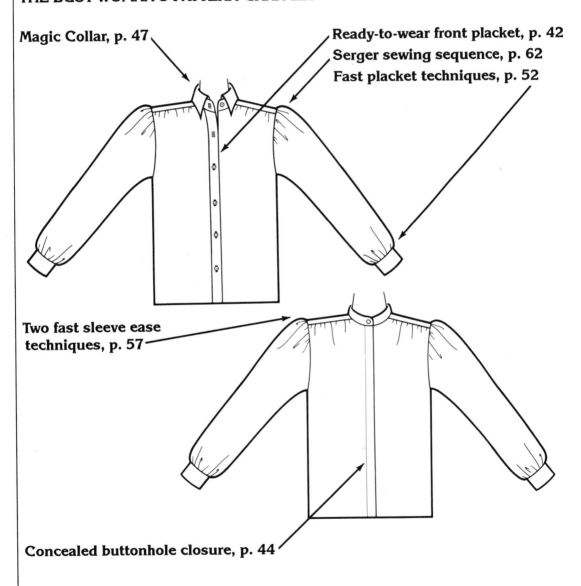

Two fast sleeve ease techniques, p. 57

Concealed buttonhole closure, p. 44

If you are juggling your schedule to make time for sewing, remember that a blouse can be made in a few hours. And those few hours of sewing can save you many dollars when compared to the price of a ready-made blouse.

This chapter will give you some ready-to-wear sewing techniques that can keep your sewing time to a minimum while giving you extremely professional results. I will show you the techniques on blouses, but remember that these techniques can be applied to your dress patterns as well.

First we'll make changes to the front opening. Then we'll change the collar and collar band. Finally we'll simplify making sleeve plackets and setting in sleeves. I'll also show you the order in which to serge a blouse and finish with a quick all-bias scarf to complement your new blouse. All these changes will free the busy woman for even more sewing.

## Two Front Openings

### Option One: Ready-to-Wear Front Placket

Any blouse or dress pattern with a placket *that buttons to the neckline* can be changed to a ready-to-wear placket, which faces, interfaces, and conceals all the raw edges of the blouse front at once. Rather than using your pattern's separate placket or facing piece, change your pattern with these simple steps. (Note: You will not need to purchase additional fabric.)

1.  Cut a tissue or wax paper extension 3 5/8" wide and as long as the garment front. Tape the extension to the center front of the pattern. Cut both blouse fronts from this new pattern piece. See Fig. 5-1.

*Buttonhole Side: Right Front*

2.  A woman's blouse has buttonholes on the right side. Therefore, on the right side, nip the neckline 1 1/4", 2 1/2", and 3 3/4" from the center edge. Nip the hemline at the same intervals, all 1 1/4" apart. See Fig. 5-2.

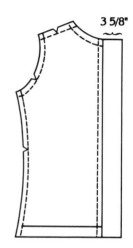

> **Don't forget to mark your pattern instructions where you want to incorporate new sewing techniques.**

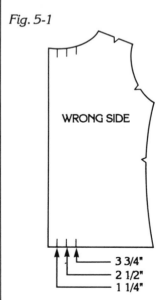

3 5/8"

*Fig. 5-1*

WRONG SIDE

3 3/4"
2 1/2"
1 1/4"

*Fig. 5-2*

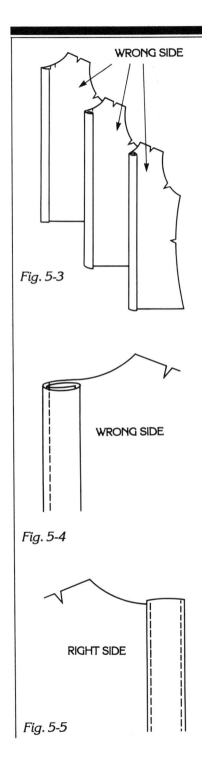

WRONG SIDE

Fig. 5-3

WRONG SIDE

Fig. 5-4

RIGHT SIDE

Fig. 5-5

3. With the wrong side of the fabric facing you, fold the blouse along the first set of nips and press. This becomes the interfacing. Fold along the second set of nips and press again. This is the facing. Fold along the third set of nips and press for the third time. This becomes the placket. See Fig. 5-3.

4. Topstitch the placket, sewing 1/4" from the outer fold (Fig. 5-4).

5. Bring the placket to the right side and complete by topstitching 1/4" from the new outer fold. See Fig. 5-5.

*Button Side: Left Front*

6. Even though the left front was cut with the 3 5/8" extension, trim away 1/2" from the *left front*. (The 1/4" placket tuck on the right front, which is formed when the placket is brought to the right side, is not needed on the button side.) See. Fig. 5-6.

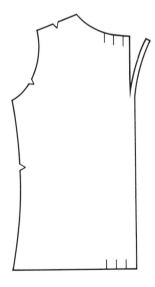

Fig. 5-6

7. Place two nips each in the neck and hemline, each measuring 1 1/4" and 2 1/2" from the center cut edge.

8. Fold along the first set of nips and press. This becomes the interfacing. Fold along the second set of nips and press. This is the facing. See Fig. 5-7.

9. Finish the button side by topstitching 1/4" from the fold. Later, when you sew on the buttons, they will hold the facing in place.

This time-saving approach gives you three layers of fabric on both left and right plackets. All the raw edges are sewn into the topstitching, with no chance of stray raw edges peeking out. See Fig. 5-8.

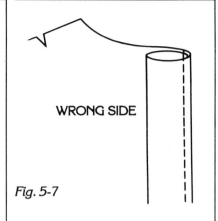

WRONG SIDE

Fig. 5-7

### Option Two: Concealed Button/Buttonhole Closure

A second placket technique conceals the button/buttonhole closure, giving a dressier look. You can easily update your favorite tailored blouse, dress, or shirt pattern with these following steps.

1. Cut a tissue or wax paper extension 5 5/8" wide and as long as the blouse front. Tape the

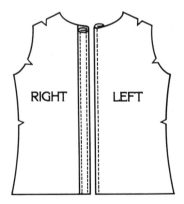

RIGHT    LEFT

Fig. 5-8

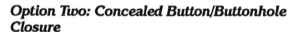
*I cut my 5 5/8" extension piece out of a non-woven fabric like Tru-Grid™. Then instead of storing the extension piece in the pattern envelope, I pin it to my sewing bulletin board and use it to change many blouse patterns.*

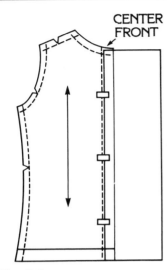

CENTER
FRONT

Fig. 5-9

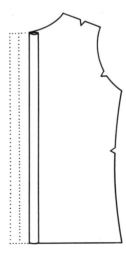

*Use the Ready-to-Wear Placket technique on menswear, too. Simply reverse the closure, making the left front for buttonholes and the right front for buttons.*

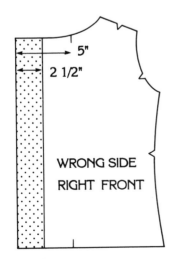

5"

2 1/2"

WRONG SIDE

RIGHT FRONT

Fig. 5-10

extension to the pattern at the *center front line.* See Fig. 5-9. Cut out both blouse fronts.

*Right Front*

2. Cut a strip of lightweight fusible interfacing 2 1/2" wide and as long as the garment front. Fuse the interfacing strip to the wrong side of the *right front,* meeting the outer edge of the blouse to the outer edge of the interfacing.

3. Working on the *wrong side* of the right front, nip the necklines 2 1/2" and 5" from the center edge. Nip the hemline at these same intervals. See Fig. 5-10.

4. Fold the blouse front along the first set of nips and press. Fold again along the second set of nips and press. See Fig. 5-11.

Fig. 5-11

5. Sew the placket by stitching 1 1/4" from the folded edge. See Fig. 5-12.

6. Press the free-floating extension to the outer fold. This free- floating extension becomes the buttonhole area. When you have sewn in the buttonholes, press the remaining fold of fabric over the buttonholes to conceal them. (See Fig. 5-14.)

*Left Front*

7. While both blouse fronts have 5 5/8" extensions, the left front does not require the concealed facing. To eliminate the extra fabric, trim off 2 1/2" from the *left front* (Fig. 5-13).

Note: Instructions 8-11 are the same as for the ready-to-wear placket in option one. See Fig. 5-7.

8. Nip the neck edge 1 1/4" and 2 1/2" from the center edge. Nip the hemline at the same intervals.

9. With the wrong side of the fabric facing you, fold the blouse along the first set of nips and press. This becomes the interfacing. Fold along the second set of nips and press again. This is the facing.

10. Topstitch the placket, sewing 1/4" from the outer fold.

11. To complete the placket, sew buttonholes in the right front's concealed placket and sew buttons on the left side. The buttons will hold the facing in place. See Fig. 5-14.

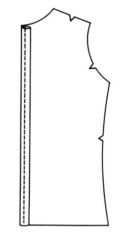

*Fig. 5-12*

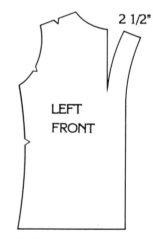

2 1/2"

LEFT FRONT

*Fig. 5-13*

**When putting buttonholes into lightweight fabrics, consider using a layer of wax paper, tissue paper, or a supportive fabric like Tear Away® or Stitch 'n Tear® underneath the buttonhole area. This supportive fabric will give the fashion fabric more weight and will prevent the buttonholes from embedding in the fabric.**

*Fig. 5-14*

## Collar Treatments

### *Magic Collar*

This unique collar treatment eliminates the bulky center-front seam and automatically places the under-collar on the bias, giving the collar greater shape. Besides looking professional, this collar is fast to sew; it's a perfect collar for the busy person.

Consider adding a Magic Collar to a tailored blouse with a lapel-type neckline or to a collar band. See Fig. 5-15. The outer edge of the collar pattern can either be curved or straight. See Fig. 5-16. To make this magical collar:

1. Cut the pattern apart at the center back (Fig. 5-17).
2. Fold under the seam allowance of the center front of *one* collar and meet it to the stitching line of the other collar center front. Pin together. See Fig. 5-18.

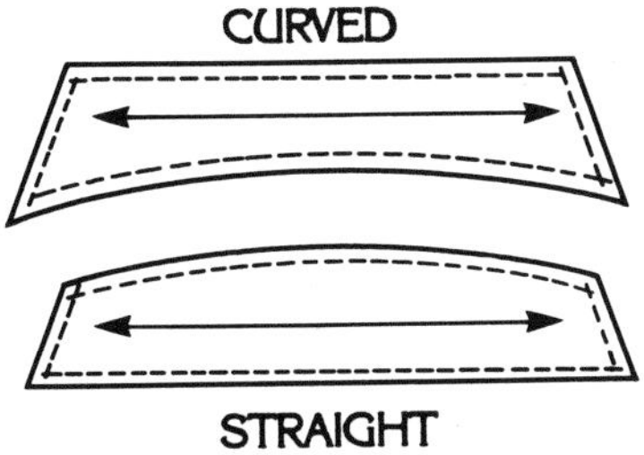

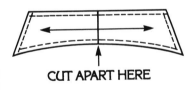

CURVED

STRAIGHT

*Fig. 5-16*

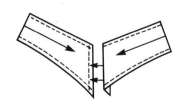

CUT APART HERE

*Fig. 5-17*

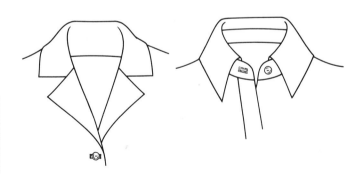

*Fig. 5-15*

*Fig. 5-18*

If using a collar with a curved outer edge, an extra triangle of seam allowance will form at the collar point. Trim off this triangle shape. See Fig. 5-19.

3. To one of the center backs, add a 5/8" seam allowance. Mark a "Place on Fold" at the other center back. See Fig. 5-19.

4. Cut out the pattern, placing the center back without a seam allowance on the fold of the fabric. (Note: If using a stripe, refold the fabric so the grain of the fabric is running horizontally.)

5. Using Chapter 3's procedure for making an interfacing pattern, trace the collar minus 1/2" seam allowances.

6. Fuse interfacing to collar. (Note: The more curved the outer edge of the collar, the more U-shaped the collar piece will be. See Fig. 5- 20.)

7. Sew center back seam. Press. See Fig. 5-21.

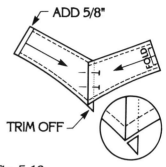

Fig. 5-19

Fig. 5-20

*If you are sewing on plain fabric, don't worry too much about the placement of the grain on the Magic Collar. I have made collars using either of the old grain lines and collars using a grain line parallel to the fold line. All seem to work fine. Only on collars with a striped fabric do you need to make the grain on the upper collar run parallel to the grain.*

Fig. 5-21

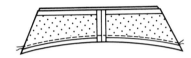

*Fig. 5-22*

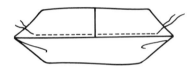

*Fig. 5-23*

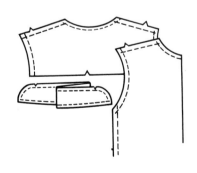

*Fig. 5-24*

8. Refold the collar, right sides together; sew outer edge (Fig. 5-22).

9. Press seam flat, then open. Grade seam allowances, trimming the undercollar seam to 1/4". Trim the excess bulk at the collar points.

10. Understitch, sewing all seam allowances to the undercollar. (Note: It will not be possible to understitch all the way to the collar points. See Fig. 5-23.)

11. Turn collar rightside out. Press.

### Collar Band

Years ago I used to avoid patterns with collar bands because my end result was a lump at the center front curves. Since then, I've learned a new technique for a bulk-free collar band. Combine this with a Magic Collar for your next tailored blouse project.

1. Since the neck edge of the collar band has an outward curve and the neck edge of the blouse has an inward curve, it is easier to sew the two contrary shapes together if you use a 1/4" seam. Therefore, trim 3/8" from the neck edge of the front, back, and collar band. Place a nip in the collar bands at the large dots along the collar edge. See Fig. 5-24.

 *When I buy material (often through mail-order), I cut a swatch and write on it (with washout marker) washing instructions, width, and yardage. It takes only a glance to know if a new pattern can be made up from what I have on hand. I do the same for trim: snip a sample, glue-stitch it to index cards, and add yardage beside the sample. Then I subtract what is used to keep it up-to-date.*

***Beth Hodges***
***Elberton, GA***

2. Usually the fusible interfacing is cut 1/8" beyond the stitching lines, but in this technique, it is cut minus the 5/8" seam allowance, to eliminate bulk and to act as a sewing guide. Cut fusible interfacing *the same size* as the finished collar bands. Fuse both collar bands. See Fig. 5-25.

3. Sandwich the collar band on each side of the neckline. Sew the bands to the garment along the neckline seam with a 1/4" seam. See Fig. 5-26.

4. Roll the center front into a cone shape until the fabric is next to the collar band (Fig. 5-27).

5. After the center front is rolled out of the way, the collar bands meet rightsides together. Sew the curve of the collar band following the interfacing edge. Stop sewing at the nip. See Fig. 5-28.

Turn the collar band to the right side and check for accuracy. If the first sewing is correct, turn wrong sides out and restitch the curve with 18-20 stitches/inch.

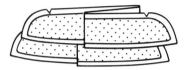

Fig. 5-25

RIGHT
SIDE

Fig. 5-26

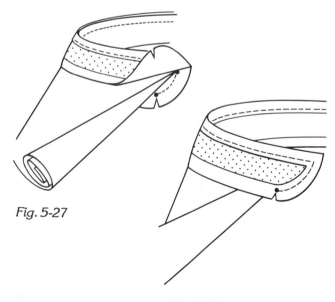

Fig. 5-27

Fig. 5-28

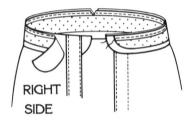
*News flash! Since we first published this book, we realized that we can make a wrapped corner on the collar band, too. Sew all the way to the front edge in Fig. 5-26. Then wrap the seam allowances down toward the inside band. Sew from the fold to the dot, as in Fig. 5-28. You'll like the results.*

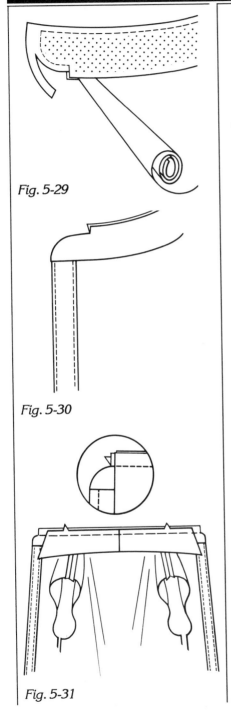

Fig. 5-29

Fig. 5-30

Fig. 5-31

6. Clip to the seam allowance at the nip. Grade seams to 1/8". If fabric ravels, secure the cut edges with Fray Check™. See Fig. 5-29.

7. Turn neck bands rightsides out and press. See Fig. 5-30. Your collar band is perfect.

### Sew Magic Collar to Collar Band.

1. Rightsides together, sew the Magic Collar to the inner collar band with a 5/8" seam. Press and grade seam allowances. See Fig. 5-31.

2. Fold under the seam allowance of the outer collar band, using the edge of the interfacing as a guide. Pin the outer collar band to the collar. Edgestitch around the collar band as shown in Fig. 5-32.

Following this procedure, your collar and collar band will be sewn completely by machine, with bulk-free results.

### Don't Forget the Wrapped Corner Collar.

The wrapped corner collar I showed you in Chapter 4 for semi-lined jackets can be used as effectively on blouses and dresses. This technique gives perfect corners and a beautifully tailored look.

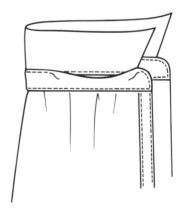

Fig. 5-32

## Two Sleeve Plackets

### *Option One: Mock Placket With a Modified Cuff*

This placket/cuff technique is terrific for beginners. Since it is similar to attaching ribbing to a T-shirt, it's a logical transition from sewing on knits to sewing on wovens.

It's also a great time-saver for pro-sewers. No one but you knows that it's not a tailored placket, which takes more time to sew.

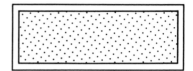

Fig. 5-33

*Cuff*

1. Create a new cuff pattern 12 1/2" X 4 1/4". This measurement fits Sizes 8-20. Interface each cuff minus 1/2" seam allowances (Fig. 5-33).

2. Rightsides together, sew the cuff into a tube. Press. See Fig. 5-34.

3. Fold each cuff in half with *wrong sides* together. Set aside. See Fig. 5-35.

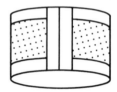

Fig. 5-34

*Sleeve*

4. In most cases, the bottom width of your sleeve pattern will exceed 12 1/4", so that the lower sleeve can be gathered or pleated. But if yours doesn't, evenly increase the bottom width by tapering from the underarm. See Fig. 5-36.

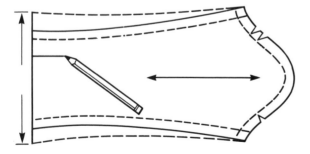

Fig. 5-36

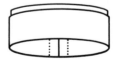

Fig. 5-35

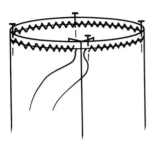

Fig. 5-37

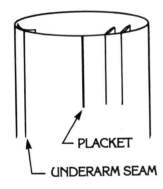

PLACKET

UNDERARM SEAM

Fig. 5-38

The side seam allowance will be 5/8" from your new cutting line.

5. With a washable marking pen or pencil, mark the placket area on the sleeve. *Do not cut the placket!*

6. Sew the underarm seam. Press.

7. Quarter and mark the lower edge of the sleeve and cuffs. If the bottom of the sleeve is wider than 12 1/4", gather the lower edge. (See Chapter 3 for an easy gathering technique.) Rightsides together, pin cuff to sleeve, matching quarter marks. Gather sleeve edge to match cuff size. See Fig. 5-37.

Note: If you prefer two or three 1/2" pleats instead of gathers, form the pleats on the far side of the placket, not between the placket and the underarm seam. See Fig. 5-38.

8. Sew the cuff to the sleeve. Grade all allowances to 1/4" and zigzag together or clean-finish with Seams Great® (Fig. 5-39).

9. On the right side, find the mark indicating the placket area. Crease cuff and sleeve along the placket line (Fig. 5-40).

10. Mark and sew a buttonhole the standard distance (1/2"-3/4") from the cuff crease,

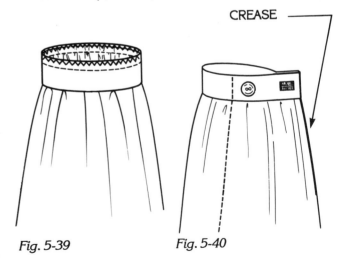

CREASE

Fig. 5-39        Fig. 5-40

sewing through all layers. Make a generous buttonhole to accommodate the many layers of fabric. Finish cuff by sewing on a button. See Figs. 5-41 and 5-42.

### Option Two: Ready-to-Wear Placket/Cuff

The next treatment takes a bit more time, but is worth it. Instead of inserting the placket in the middle of the lower sleeve fabric, we switch the underarm seam and use its natural opening for the placket. This allows you to finish the placket and cuff entirely by machine.

*Sleeve Changes*

1. Draw a line through the center of your pattern's placket, from sleeve cap to bottom of sleeve, parallel to the grain line.

2. Mark two hash marks on the new seamline, at the top of the placket and in the middle of the seam. When we cut the pattern apart on the new seamline, these hash marks will serve as notches. See Fig. 5-43.

3. Cut the sleeve along the new seamline. Place the old *stitching lines* at the underarms on top of each other.

4. Add a 5/8" seam allowance on both sides of the new seam with tissue or wax paper. See Fig. 5-44.

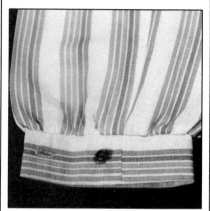

*Fig. 5-41*

*Fig. 5-42*

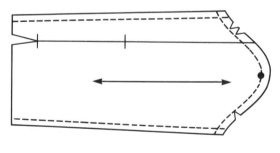

*Fig. 5-43*

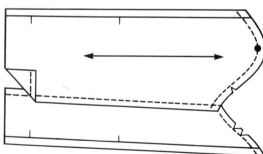

*Fig. 5-44*

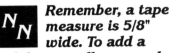
**Remember, a tape measure is 5/8" wide. To add a quick seam allowance, lay your tape measure next to the sewing line and trace.**

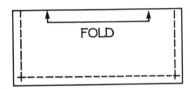

FOLD

*Fig. 5-46*

5. Cut the sleeves out of the fashion fabric.

6. Zigzag, serge, or clean finish the raw edges of the seam with Seams Great®. The seam will double as the placket, so this extra finish is needed. (The underarm/placket seam will be sewn *after* the cuff is attached.)

7. Following your pattern instructions, either gather or sew tucks at the lower edge of the sleeve. See Fig. 5-45.

*Cuff Changes*

8. If the cuff has seam allowances all around the pattern, eliminate the outer edge seam by placing the cuff on the lengthwise fold of the fabric. You will now have one piece of fabric for the cuff instead of two, a time-saver. You have also removed bulk from the corner of the cuff. See Fig. 5-46.

Stabilize each cuff with fusible interfacing. Fuse the entire cuff, minus 1/2" seam allowances (Fig. 5-47).

9. Rightsides together, sew the cuff side seams. Grade, press, and turn rightside out.

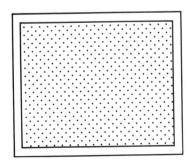

*Fig. 5-47*

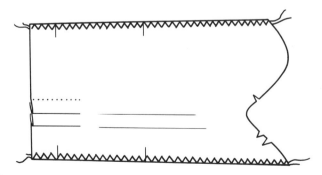

*Fig. 5-45*

*Attach Cuff to Sleeve*

10. Rightsides together, pin cuff to sleeve, with the 5/8" seam allowances of the sleeve extending beyond both sides of the cuff.

11. Securely wrap the sleeve's 5/8" seam allowances around the cuff. Pin in place. When the cuff is sewn, pressed, and turned rightside out, the seam allowance will be encased in the cuff. However, if the seam allowance is not securely wrapped around the cuff, the finished placket edge will not be flush with the cuff. See Fig. 5-48.

12. Sew cuff to the lower edge of the sleeve. Trim all layers to 1/4". Zigzag the raw edges together, using a close zigzag stitch. (You can also finish the raw edges with Seams Great® or by serging.) See Fig. 5-48.

13. Match notches and sew the underarm seam. Stop sewing at the notch at the top of the placket. Press open the seam and turn the sleeve rightside out (Fig. 5-49).

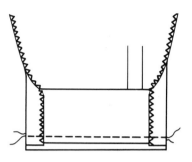

Fig. 5-48

Fig. 5-49

 *I involve my boys (8 and 10) in my sewing. Each one wants to sit by my side and help me sew. When I'm cutting, they are sewing on paper, so I'm not feeling as if I'm taking time away. Instead, they are learning to appreciate the finer things hand- made. Anyone can buy things, but one who really cares makes things, a good lesson for today's kids. (P.S. Having a very supportive husband who will make dinner when I'm sewing helps!)*

**Alverea Bizjack**
**Kent, WA**

## Easing and Setting in Sleeves

### Checking Sleeve Ease

The average ease in set-in sleeves is 1-1 1/2" for wovens and 1" for knits. Be sure to check your pattern, especially if you are sewing more difficult fabrics that don't ease well. Measure the sleeve armhole sewing line between the notches. Then measure the blouse armhole sewing line. If your pattern has more than the average ease, reduce the excess with this technique.

1. Place wax or tissue paper over the sleeve pattern. Outline the cutting line of the cap.

2. Measure down 3/8" from the cutting line at the top of the sleeve and put a dot. Redraw the sleeve cap, gradually tapering from the 3/8" mark to the cutting line at each notch. See Fig. 5-50. Use the new line as your cutting line.

### Matching Notches

Notches are used to tell the front from the back of the sleeve, one notch denoting the front, two notches denoting the back. Notches do not always match.

Check your pattern by measuring the distance from the underarm seam to each notch. Are these measure-

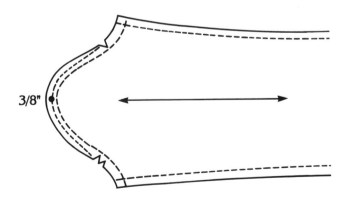

3/8"

*Fig. 5-50*

ments the same for both the sleeve and the bodice? Sometimes the measurement is off by 1/4" or more.

When setting in a sleeve, use the notches as they were intended: to tell which pieces go together and to tell the front from the back. If the notches don't meet, don't force them to meet.

### Easing a Sleeve

Rather than sew two rows of basting threads to ease a sleeve, I prefer either of these two time-saving techniques. My choice is determined by the weight of the fabric.

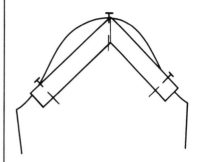

*Fig. 5-51*

#### Seams Great® Easing

Seams Great® is 40-denier tricot cut into bias strips. The 1 1/4" width is generally used to create bulk-free casing and to help ease sleeves. Since Seams Great® is lightweight, it cannot be used to ease every sleeve, only those of light- to medium-weight blouse or dress fabric.

1. Cut 1 1/4" wide Seams Great® the length of the bodice armhole from notch, across shoulder, to notch.

2. Use three pins to pin the Seams Great® to the wrong side of the sleeve, matching raw edges at the notches and cap. See Fig. 5-51.

3. Set the machine at the standard stitch length. Stretch the Seams Great® to meet the sleeve and sew the two layers together 1/2" from the cut edge. The Seams Great®will retract to its original size, automatically causing the sleeve to ease. See Fig. 5-52. Since you sewed the Seams Great® to the underside, it does not show. (Attention, mothers and teachers: This is a great easing technique to teach your beginners.)

#### Finger Easing

1. Set the machine for 8-10 stitches per inch for light- to medium-weight fabric; 6 stitches per inch for heavyweight fabrics.

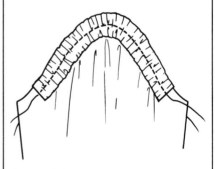

*Fig. 5-52*

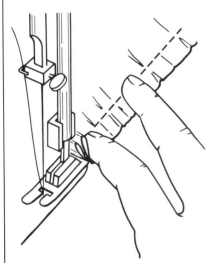

Fig. 5-53 Finger easing

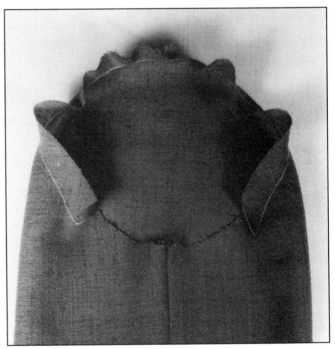

*Sleeves are drafted to fit smoothly without gathers at the very top of the cap. Therefore, when sewing a dress or blouse sleeve, do not ease stitch for 1/2" on each side of the top of the cap. When sewing a jacket sleeve, however, ease the entire cap.*

2. Sew a row of straight stitching 1/2" from the cut edge, between the notches. To create the easing, place a finger behind the presser foot, meeting your finger to the back of the presser foot. While sewing, try to stop the fabric from flowing behind the presser foot. Fabric will collect between the presser foot and your finger.

3. Sew 2-3" and release your finger. Repeat. See Fig. 5-53. Although it is impossible to prevent the flow of fabric behind the presser foot, this finger easing causes the feed dogs to ease the fabric slightly (Fig. 5-54).

### Setting in Sleeves

1. Pin the sleeve into the armhole, matching the underarm seams to each other and matching the large dot at the cap with the shoulder seam.

Fig. 5-54

If your finger easing is too tight, clip an easing stitch. If your easing is too loose, pull the easing thread tighter.

2.  Plan your sewing so that you will stitch the underarm area twice. Start sewing at the notch farthest from you. Sew the armhole with a 5/8" seam. When you reach the starting point, restitch the underarm area with a 3/8" seam allowance.

3.  Trim the underarm seam to the 3/8" stitching line. Leave the rest of the seam allowance at 5/8". See Fig. 5-55.

4.  Press the seams flat to set the stitches, pressing over a ham or Tailor Board®. *Never press the sleeve from the right side, because it would flatten the roll of the cap.*

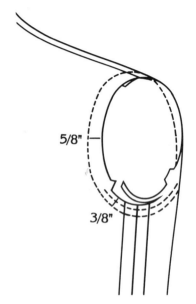

5/8"

3/8"

Fig. 5-55

 *My sister made me a board that's 2'x2'. It has 49 3" dowels. Each dowel holds a spool of thread and a bobbin with matching thread, ready to sew.*

*Another time-saver that works well for me: I have a card table on my left with a framed bulletin board on it. When I have something to gather, such as a sleeve to an armband or a skirt to a waistband, I divide the band into four parts and using quilting pins, attach the band to the board. After running the gathering thread on the garment and dividing it into four parts, I match the marks on both pieces, secure them with quilting pins, and then pull up the gathers. The material pinned to the bulletin board makes it easier to place the gathers evenly.*

*Maude Hansen*
*Alto, MI*

## Gathered Sleeves

In Chapter 4, I showed you how to give a jacket sleeve a finished look with a sleeve head. Similar help is needed by the gathered sleeve common to many blouses and dresses. A sleeve head keeps the gathers pronounced and prevents the sleeve from drooping.

A gathered sleeve is usually gathered halfway between the notch and cap on each side. Before gathering, add a stabilizing fabric to the sleeve cap. For knit fabrics, use polyester fleece; for wovens, use a double layer of bridal illusion (veiling fabric). See Fig. 5-56.

1. Trace a pattern for the sleeve head by placing wax or tissue paper over the cap of the sleeve pattern. Outline the cap and measure down 2" from the dot. Taper this line to the gather dots. Cut the stabilizing fabrics this size. Clean finish the raw edges of the bridal illusion by zigzagging, serging, or with 5/8"-wide Seams Great®. See Fig. 5-57.

2. Pin the stabilizing fabric to the wrong side of the sleeve.

3. Gather the sleeve, using the easy gathering technique given in Chapter 3. This time,

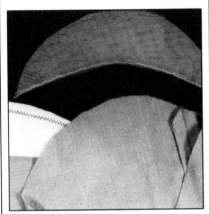

Fig. 5-56

 *I tuck in most of my blouses, so I don't waste time hemming the bottoms. Instead, I serge them.*

**Robbie**

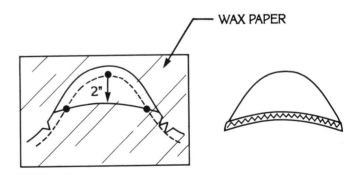

WAX PAPER

Fig. 5-57

however, you will gather both the fashion fabric and the stabilizing fabric as one. See Fig. 5-58.

4. Set in the sleeve. The added fabric will keep the gathers pronounced, even through washings. See Fig. 5-59.

## Serger Blouse Construction

Combine the speed sewing of a serger and the straight stitch of a conventional machine to sew yet another professional-looking blouse in less time. Many of the Busy Woman's sewing techniques you learned earlier also apply to the serger.

Use these speed sewing techniques on shirt or blouse patterns that require a minimum of easing in the sleeve cap. Use a 3/4- or 4/2-thread serger; either 4-thread serger seam is secure enough for woven fabrics (Fig. 5-60). Be sure to test your serged seam on a fabric scrap. If stitches pull apart on the right side of the fabric, adjust the tensions or shorten the stitch length until you have a more secure seam. If there is an area of the garment that receives excess stress, such as underarm seams, reinforce that seam with a row of conventional machine stitching.

When making interfacing patterns for collars, cuffs, and facings, cut the interfacing to end 1/2" from the cutting line. Since excess seam allowances will be cut off by serging, mark the notches, dots, and any other

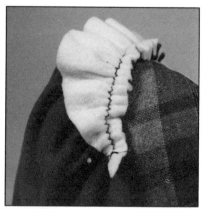

Fig. 5-58

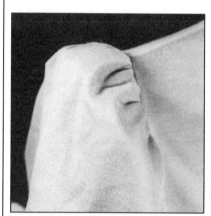

Fig. 5-59

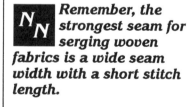 **Remember, the strongest seam for serging woven fabrics is a wide seam width with a short stitch length.**

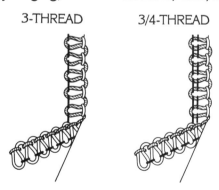

3-THREAD          3/4-THREAD

Fig. 5-60

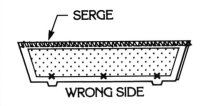

SERGE

WRONG SIDE

Fig. 5-61

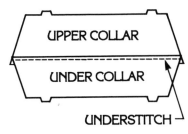

UPPER COLLAR

UNDER COLLAR

UNDERSTITCH

Fig. 5-62

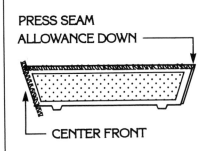

PRESS SEAM
ALLOWANCE DOWN

CENTER FRONT

Fig. 5-63

markings on the seam line, rather than on the cutting line, using a water-erasable pen or tailor's chalk.

Here's the serging sequence for a blouse.

1. Rightsides of under- and uppercollar together, serge the outer edge seam of the collar. See Fig. 5-61.

2. Press the seam allowance flat. Then press it toward the undercollar and understitch with a conventional sewing machine (Fig. 5-62).

3. Fold the collar rightsides together. (The seam allowance is wrapped toward the undercollar.) Serge the center front collar seams. Press the seams flat. Turn the collar rightside out. Press. See Fig. 5-63.

4. Serge the shoulder seams.

5. Pin the collar to the neckline, matching notches, dots, and center back.

6. Pin the front facing to the neckline seam. The collar will be sandwiched between the garment and the facing. Do not pin the center front edge of the facing and garment. See Fig. 5-64.

Note: On some shirts, the front facing is cut with the shirt front as one piece, instead of a shirt front with a

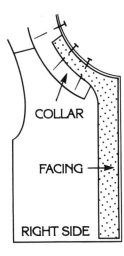

COLLAR

FACING

RIGHT SIDE

Fig. 5-64

separate facing. If your shirt has this type of built-in facing, simply fold it on the foldline, rightsides together. Sandwich the collar between the garment and the facing. Omit step 8.

7. Serge the neckline seam. Press the seam flat. Press the seam allowance to the garment side.

8. Wrap the seam allowance at the center front neck edge to the garment side. Serge the center front seam. Press seam flat. See Fig. 5-65.

9. Turn the facing rightside out, folding on the seam line. Press along the seam line.

10. Finish the hem of the sleeve. Use the flatlock stitch on the serger, or use a conventional sewing machine to hem the sleeve.

11. Pin the sleeve to the armhole, matching notches. Serge the seam. See Fig. 5-66.

12. Pin the sleeve and underarm seam together. Be sure that the bottom edge of the sleeve hem is even. Serge the seam. See Fig. 5-67.

13. Finish the hem as desired. Follow the pattern instructions to finish the garment.

 *I subscribe to home-sewing catalogs, which provides me with a means of determining which patterns I am interested in, so that I can avoid the time-consuming task of reviewing patterns at the sewing centers.*

*Also, after I purchase a pattern, I Xerox it, because I maintain a book of all patterns I have. Then when I go to the sewing store, I have quick reference to all my patterns, showing the amount of material and notions I need to purchase.*

**Sharon Bates**
**Tequesta, FL**

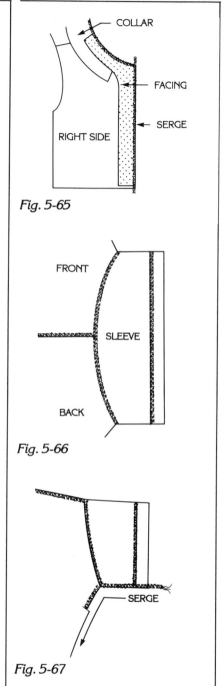

*Fig. 5-65*

*Fig. 5-66*

*Fig. 5-67*

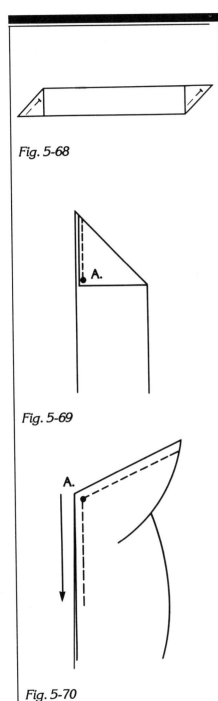

Fig. 5-68

Fig. 5-69

Fig. 5-70

## All-Bias Scarf

Using ready-to-wear know-how, in ten minutes or less--honest!--you can create a bias scarf or sash out of a length of fabric that is only 6-9" wide. Tie it into a bow, sailor's knot, or ascot, and you have a quick accent for your new blouse.

### Determine the Scarf Size.

The key to making this scarf is that *the fabric length must be evenly divisible by the fabric width.* Suggested rectangle sizes are: 6"x60", 7"x49", 8"x56", 9"x54".

When deciding upon the scarf size, keep in mind that the scarf will be approximately one-third shorter and narrower than the starting size. If you start with a rectangle 6"x60", the *finished* scarf will be 4"x40".

1. Mark the center of your long strip with a pin. Then rightsides together, fold one corner in half and pin. Repeat for the opposite corner. See Fig. 5-68.

2. Start at the point of one corner and sew raw edges together with a 1/4" seam allowance. Stop sewing 1/4" before raw edges end (A). Leave the needle in the fabric at A. See Fig. 5-69.

3. With the needle in the fabric, raise the presser foot and meet the horizontal and vertical raw edges together. The fabric will begin to twist. Lower the presser foot and continue sewing the horizontal and vertical raw edges together until you reach the middle of the scarf. The fabric will continue to twist and turn as you sew. See Fig. 5-70.

4. Repeat steps 2 and 3 on the opposite end of the scarf, but stop sewing 2" from the middle, leaving an opening for turning the scarf rightsides out.

5. Before turning, press seam allowances to one side.

6. Turn rightside out and close opening with hand stitches. Magic! You have an all-bias scarf! (Fig. 5-71

## Short-Cut Blouse (Fig. 5-72)

My friends at Minnesota Fabrics designed the perfect "blouse" for the woman too busy to sew an entire blouse. Actually, it is a false blouse front. Keep your jacket buttoned and no one will ever know you cheated.

You will need 1 1/4" yards of 45"-wide blouse fabric.

1. Enlarge the pattern from the graph. See Fig. 5-73.

2. Cut two pieces from the pattern. Remember to cut on the bias.

3. Rightsides together, sew the two pieces with a 1/4" seam allowance, leaving a 3" opening between A and B. Grade seams, trim corners, and clip curves as necessary.

4. Turn rightside out and press. Slip-stitch opening closed or place a strip of Stitch Witchery® in the opening and fuse it closed.

To wear, cross the long ends behind the back of the neck, bring to the front, and tie as desired. Be sure to keep your jacket buttoned!

*Fig. 5-71*

*Fig. 5-72*

*Fig. 5-73*

ONE SQUARE = 2"

# CHAPTER 6
# READY-TO-WEAR TECHNIQUES FOR CASUAL TOPS

## THE BUSY WOMAN'S PATTERN CHANGES

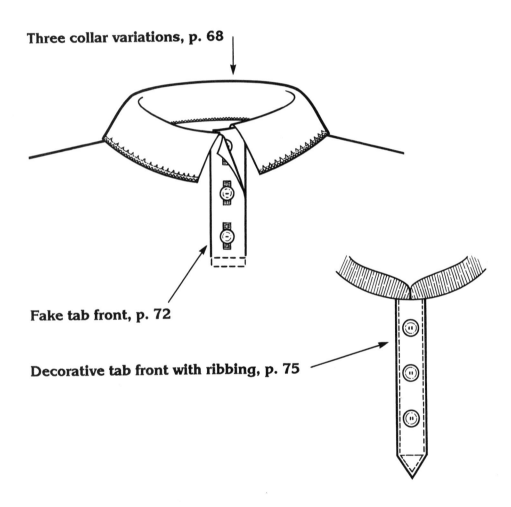

Three collar variations, p. 68

Fake tab front, p. 72

Decorative tab front with ribbing, p. 75

Casual tops can extend the versatility of a skirt or a pair of slacks. They are perfect wardrobe extenders and can be worn for many occasions. In short, casual tops are a must for a busy woman's wardrobe. And with my simplified techniques, you will be able to sew a casual top in a matter of hours.

The two construction areas that require special attention on a classic styled casual top are the tab front and the collar. In this chapter, you will learn an easy tab-front technique and some novel ways to give collars that purchased ready-to-wear look. Let's start with the collar treatments.

## Three Collar Treatments

### Scalloped Collar (Fig. 6-1)

If you have decorative stitches on your sewing machine, here's the perfect place to use them

1. Fuse interfacing to the wrong side of the collar. Interface the entire piece. See Fig. 6-2.

2. Meet *wrong sides* together. Do not sew any seams. Place a layer of supportive fabric like Tear Away®, Stitch 'n Tear®, or paper under the fabric. The supportive fabric is needed to

 *For best results, read your pattern instructions and mark the sewing changes you want to make after reading this chapter.*

 *These collar treatments work best on interlock or your body fabric. Don't use ribbing for the collars, though. It would stretch out of shape.*

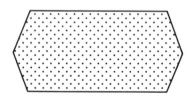

Fig. 6-2

 *Use applique scissors if possible. This wonderful tool trims extremely accurately, since the guard on the blade prevents cutting of the fashion fabric.*

Fig. 6-1

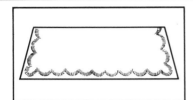

Fig. 6-3

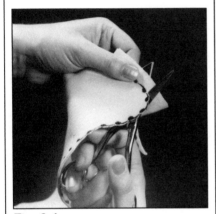

Fig. 6-4

prevent the fabric from stretching out of shape as you sew.

3. Set your machine for a decorative scallop stitch. Stitch around the collar on the 5/8" seam allowance. Note: Please check the stitch length and thread tensions on a scrap of fabric to determine the best stitching setting for your fabric. See Fig. 6-3.

4. Tear away the supportive fabric and trim away the excess fabric outside the decorative stitching. See Fig. 6-4.

### Ready-to-Wear Look-Alike Collar (Fig. 6-5)

This technique yields a collar that closely resembles a purchased collar. In order to sew it, you will need a blind-hem stitch on your sewing machine. )

1. Interface the collar from the neck edge to 1/2" from the outer fold. The interfacing is eliminated from the fold, so that the decorative stitches will flute the edge, making it look like many ready-to-wear collars. See Fig. 6-6.

2. Sew the collar together as directed on the pattern guide. Turn rightside out and press.

3. To give that ready-to-wear look to the outer edges, sew two rows of stitches using a

Fig. 6-5

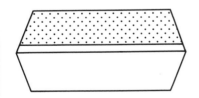

Fig. 6-6

contrasting thread (machine-embroidery thread will give additional luster). Lock your stitches at beginning and end.

Sew the first row with a medium width zigzag (2-3) and a short length (1). Sew over the outer folded edge with the "zig" off the fold and the "zag" in the fabric. Do not sew the two center front edges.

Sew the second row over the zigzag stitches, using a blind-hem stitch with a wide width (4) and the same short length (1). If possible on your machine, use the right-needle position. When sewing, the straight stitch should be stitching off the fabric and the "zag" of the blind-hem stitch should stitch into the collar. See Fig. 6-7.

If your machine is equipped with a stretch blind-hem stitch, use one row of it in place of two rows of stitching.

The combination of these two rows of stitching will create a collar resembling a rugby-styled collar. See Fig. 6-8.

An alternate way to create the same look is to use decorative threads like pearl cotton or topstitching thread in a 3-thread serger. Serge the outer edge of the collar for this decorative look. See Fig. 6-9.

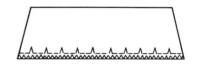

Fig. 6-7

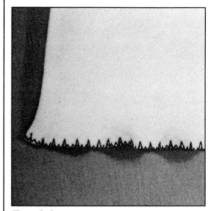

Fig. 6-8

Fig. 6-9

Fig. 6-10

## Tailored Look Collar (Fig. 6-10)

1. Interface the entire collar. Sew as the pattern guide instructs. Then turn rightside out and press.

2. Place a layer of tissue paper, wax paper, or other supportive fabric underneath the collar. Set your machine at a satin stitch, widest width and short length.

Note: Please check the zigzag stitch settings on a scrap of fabric to determine the best stitch length for your fabric.

3. Using a contrasting thread, stitch over the outer fold. As with the last collar treatment, the "zig" of the stitch should go off the fabric's fold.

4. If desired, sew an additional row of satin stitches approximately 1/2" from the first row (Fig. 6-11).

5. Remove supportive fabric and the collar is complete.

 *I work full-time outside my home and have two little ones, so that leaves me little time to sew. I get up an hour earlier each morning to sew. It's surprising what you can do in an hour of peace and quiet.*

*I use multi-size patterns, which means tracing. I find tracing the whole pattern instead of half ultimately saves me time. If I need two or more of one pattern piece, I make them. It takes a little longer, but the time saved in cutting and reusing of the pattern saves time in the long run.*

**Nancy Greenwalt**
**Ritzville, WA**

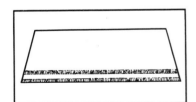

Fig. 6-11

## Two Tab Fronts

### *Fake Tab Front*

Traditional tab front plackets are not always easy to sew. Before I developed the Fake Tab Front technique, my greatest difficulty was getting the bottom of the tab perfectly square, without puckers.

Then I tried changing the tab opening to a fake tab. To my delight, it eliminated puckered corners and neatly finished the neckline. Here's how to make it yourself.

1. When cutting out the garment pattern, place the center front on the fold. Cut out the pattern. Do not cut the fabric along the placket opening, as sometimes instructed on the pattern guide.

2. With a washable marking pen, mark the center front on the *wrong side* of the garment. Still on the wrong side, mark a tab-front opening 3/4" to the *left* of the center front. Draw an opening 6" long and parallel to the center front. Make 1/4" nips in the neckline seam allowance at the center front and tab line. See Fig. 6-12.

3. Make a new tab pattern. Place a length of wax or tissue paper over the front pattern piece. With a marking pen, outline the new tab piece, using these dimensions (Fig. 6-13):

   • Extend the center front 1".

   • Outline the neck cutting line.

   • Outline the shoulder cutting line for 2 1/2".

   • Make the front placket 7" long.

   • Draw the bottom 4 1/2" wide.

   • Connect the shoulder cutting line to the bottom with a slight arch.

4. Cut out the new tab pattern by placing the center front on the fold. See Fig. 6-14. Generally, the tab and collar are in a solid color that contrasts or coordinates with the main

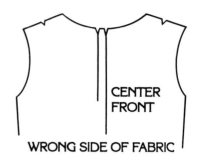

CENTER FRONT

WRONG SIDE OF FABRIC

*Fig. 6-12*

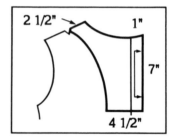

*Fig. 6-13*

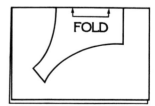

FOLD

*Fig. 6-14*

*Fig. 6-15*

fashion fabric. Interface the entire tab facing with a light-weight fusible interfacing.

5. On the wrong side of the tab, mark the center front. Mark the tab opening 3/4" to the left of the center. Make the opening 6" long and parallel to the center front. See Fig. 6-15.

6. Rightsides together, meet the tab piece to the garment, matching the *tab lines*. Note: When the two tab lines are stacked on top of one another, the shoulder areas will not match exactly. One shoulder area will almost match; the other will be completely awry.

7. Stitch a line 1/8" from the tab line on both sides, sewing to a point at the end of the tab. At the point, sew with 15-18 stitches/inch to reinforce the seam. See Fig. 6-16.

8. Cut along the tab front opening. Turn the tab to the wrong side. Press. See Fig. 6-17.

9. Sew the front and back together at the shoulder seams. Do not catch the tab in these seams. When using knit fabrics, the shoulder seams should be stabilized to prevent stretching, using one of these techniques:

- If your fashion fabric is lightweight, cut a 1/2" strip of fashion fabric along the *straight-of-grain*. Sew this strip into the shoulder seam (a ready-to-wear technique).

GARMENT RIGHT    GARMENT LEFT

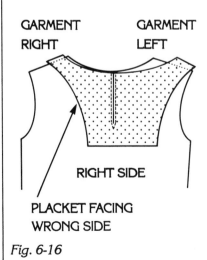

RIGHT SIDE

PLACKET FACING WRONG SIDE

*Fig. 6-16*

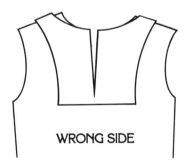

WRONG SIDE

*Fig. 6-17*

- Sew pre-shrunk cotton twill tape or nylon Stay-Tape™ into the seam.

10. Pin the collar to the neckline. Meet the *right* collar edge to the center front nip of the garment. Meet the *left* collar edge even with the nip on the tab. See Fig. 6-18.

11. Flip the tab facing to the outside. Match the right and left shoulders of the tab facing to the shoulder seams of the garment. Pin together. The collar is sandwiched between the two. On the garment's *left* side, forcing the tab to meet the shoulder will automatically form the tab to fold back on itself and form a placket. See Fig. 6-19.

12. Sew the neckline. Be careful to separate the left and right sides as you sew. Grade the seam allowances and turn rightside out.

13. To complete the fake tab front, sew across the bottom as illustrated in Fig. 6-20.

14. To complete the back neckline, sew the seam allowances to the garment using a zigzag or serpentine stitch. Trim the collar seams to this stitching. Machine or hand catch the shoulder tab to the shoulder seam.

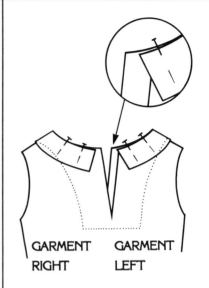

GARMENT     GARMENT
RIGHT       LEFT

Fig. 6-18

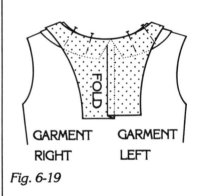

GARMENT     GARMENT
RIGHT       LEFT

Fig. 6-19

Fig. 6-20

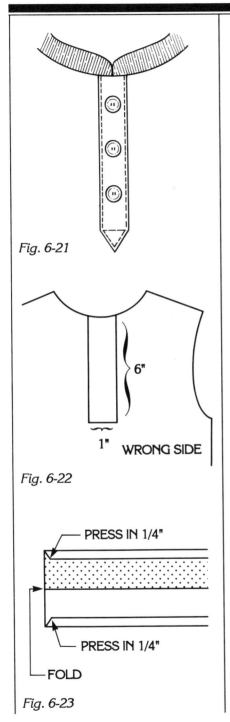

Fig. 6-21

Fig. 6-22

6"

1"  WRONG SIDE

PRESS IN 1/4"

PRESS IN 1/4"

FOLD

Fig. 6-23

### Decorative Tab Front With Ribbing (Fig. 6-21)

This tab front technique takes a little more sewing time, but the result will be both decorative and functional. Notice the triangular accent at the bottom of the tab. Believe it or not, this triangle forms all by itself.

Add this decorative accent to a casual top, T-shirt, or sweatshirt. Use contrasting woven fabric for an extra embellishment. The neckline can also be finished with a collar instead of ribbing.

1. Decide on a finished placket width and length. A common size on casual tops is 1" wide and 6-7" long.

2. Mark the finished placket size on the center front of the wrong side of the garment. See Fig. 6-22.

3. Cut the placket strip from a contrasting color, using these dimensions:

   - Width: Double the finished placket width plus 1/2" for seam allowances.

   - Length: Double the finished placket length plus the finished width of the placket.

For the pictured placket, which is 1" wide by 6" long, the placket strip would be 2 1/2" wide by 13" long.

4. Cut a strip of fusible interfacing the width of the finished placket and double the length of the finished placket (e.g., 1" wide by 12" long).

5. Fold the placket in half lengthwise, wrong sides together; press.

6. Open the placket; place the strip of fusible interfacing along the fold of the placket and fuse in place. Press in the 1/4" seam allowances on the long sides. See Fig. 6-23.

7. On the garment, cut down the center of the placket, stopping 1/2" from the bottom. Cut to the points of both corners, forming a triangle. Apply a seam sealant such as Fray Check™ to

the corners. Trim the seam allowances to 1/4"
from the plackets lines. See Fig.6-24.

8. Open the placket area on the shirt front so that
the cut edges form a straight line (Fig. 6-25).

9. Place one long edge of the placket along the
placket area of the shirt, rightsides together and
shirt side toward you. Stitch the placket to the
garment, using a 1/4" seam allowance and
stitching along the markings you made in step
2. When you reach the clipped points, which
will become the bottom of the finished placket,
reinforce the area with another line of stitching.
See Fig. 6-25.

10. Press the seam flat, then toward the placket.

11. Cut ribbing as wide as your pattern indicates,
but don't sew it into a circle. Fold the ribbing in
half the long way, wrong sides together.
Quarter the neckline and the ribbing. Pin the
ribbing to the neckline, meeting raw edges and
quarter marks. At the center fronts, pull the
*folded edge* of the ribbing up to the raw edge
of the neckline (Fig. 6-26). The raw edges of

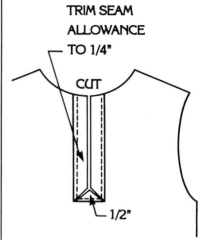

Fig. 6-24

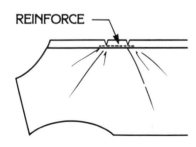

Fig. 6-25

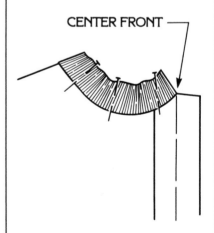

Fig. 6-26

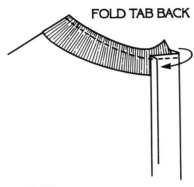

FOLD TAB BACK

Fig. 6-27

the ribbing will extend above the neckline, but will be trimmed off after sewing the neckline seam.

12. Fold the placket back on itself along the foldline, meeting rightsides of the placket together. The center front of the ribbing is now sandwiched between the placket front and back. See Fig. 6-27.

13. Sew the ribbing to the shirt. At the same time, you will finish the top of the placket. Press the seam toward the garment. Trim off the excess ribbing at the neckline. Turn the placket rightside out.

14. Finish the placket by edgestitching the remaining long edge of the placket in place,

*I'm proud of the way I use my lunch hour at work to mend and sew creatively. I take a totebag containing a needle, pins, fold-up scissors, and a spool of thread. At lunch time I eat and read for 20-30 minutes, then spend the rest of the hour sewing. If it's nice outside, I sit in the local park. Natural sunlight is wonderful for sewing! If not, I get a window seat in the company lounge. I am allowed to combine my two 15- minute breaks with my lunch hour, so I end up getting 1 1/2 hours of quiet pleasure every day. I find that lunch-hour sewing gives me an almost daily time slot, my projects don't pile up, I don't spend money shopping, and I don't overeat--a winning combination!*

**Cindy Boden**
**Noblesville, IN**

sewing from the rightside of the placket so the topstitching will be accurate. See Fig. 6-28.

15. Lap the placket over itself. A triangle will form naturally at the bottom of the placket. Note: On a woman's shirt, the placket should lap right over left; on a man's, left over right. To hold the placket in place, topstitch the triangular area. See Fig. 6-29.

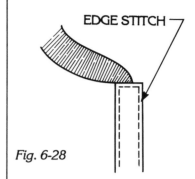

EDGE STITCH

*Fig. 6-28*

 ***One of my married daughters lives 80 miles away and we plan on visiting each other once a month. Since she enjoys sewing as much as I do, we decided to make the visit do double-duty. A week before a visit, we discuss our sewing projects on the phone, planning what we'll need. We try to have everything ready beforehand. Then we spend one day of a visiting weekend strictly on our sewing. We try out new techniques, solve problems, and learn together. Sometimes we exchange our work and get a great deal of pleasure sewing for the other. At the end of the weekend, we find we have usually accomplished a great deal--not only of sewing and mending, but more important to us, a monthly renewal of our personal mother-daughter love relationship.***

***June Coward***
***Miami Springs, FL***

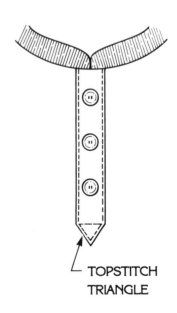

TOPSTITCH
TRIANGLE

*Fig. 6-29*

# CHAPTER 7

# SKIRTS AND SLACKS--A FRESH APPROACH

### THE BUSY WOMAN'S PATTERN CHANGES

"Hand-picked" zipper all by machine, p. 84
Fitted-looking elasticized waistband, p. 90
Hidden pocket closure, p. 82

Two-seam fly front zipper, p. 86
Easy belt loops, p. 89

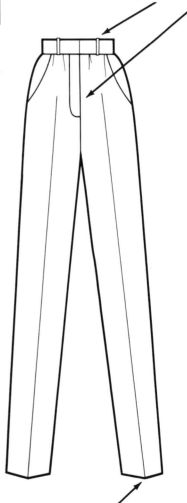

Quick and accurate pressing techniques for creases, p. 80

After our son Ted has been tucked into bed and my husband Rich has fallen asleep on the couch, I sneak away to my sewing room and enjoy a few hours of uninterrupted sewing. Since my sewing hours are limited and must not be wasted, I have found these techniques for skirts and slacks extremely efficient.

This chapter, like the others, is written in sewing sequence: e.g., the zipper instructions are given prior to waistband techniques. I usually finish all edges of my slacks and skirts before I sew them together.

## Slacks

### Determine the Front Crease.

Before sewing one stitch in your slacks, establish the front crease. This is the easiest time to press the crease because you do not have interfering seams. Oddly, this step is usually ignored on pattern guides, even though you can more accurately position the flat pieces of fabric.

1. Fold each slacks front with the wrong sides together, matching the cut edges of the hem and crotch. The cut edges between the crotch and hem may not meet, due to the shaping of the leg. Do not force the edges between the hem and crotch to meet. See Fig. 7-1.

2. Press the crease between the crotch and hem. Permanently set the crease by pressing five seconds with a steam iron and press cloth (or iron plate if needed). Lift the iron and pound with a Tailor Clapper® (9" x 2 1/2" hardwood specially designed to flatten and crease). Pounding with the clapper forces out the moisture and creates a sharp, long-lasting crease. Let the slacks front dry five to ten minutes, to assure a sharp crease. The back crease will be pressed after the legs are sewn together.

*I know you will want to add these time-saving techniques to your sewing skills. Read your pattern instructions and mark the procedures you want to change.*

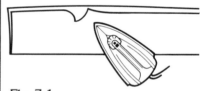

*Fig. 7-1*

*I like to make two pairs of slacks at once. While the front creases are drying, a second pair can also be pressed. It really doesn't take too much longer to sew two pairs.*

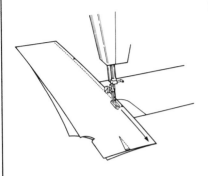

Fig. 7-2

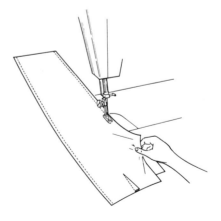

## Slacks Seam Hints

### Outer Side Seams

Rightsides together, sew the front and back legs together at the outer side seam. Press the seam flat to straighten the stitches and then press it open over a sleeve roll to prevent the seam edges from leaving an imprint on the right side. See Fig. 7-2.

### Inseam

In a quality slacks pattern, the back inseam will always be 1/2" shorter than the front inseam. Since the back crotch area is curved, it forms a bias. This bias area will stretch as you ease the back to the front. In turn, this simple easing will give you a smoother fit in the back thigh and extra fabric in the front leg area for sitting ease.

1. Match the cut edges from the hem to the knee. (The pattern's knee is the halfway point of the inseam.)
2. Sew from the hem to the knee with the fabric raw edges meeting. At the knee, stretch the back inseam to meet the front inseam and continue to sew the remaining half of the inseam. See Fig. 7-3.

**For best results, use ease stitching, sewing with the longer seam next to the feed dogs and the shorter seam under the presser foot. See Chapter 3 for further reference.**

Fig. 7-3

### Determine the Back Crease.

1. Press the seam allowance, using the sleeve roll. Turn each leg rightside out.

2. Fold the slacks along the pressed front crease and anchor the front crease with a sleeve board or other sewing/pressing tools to prevent the slacks from shifting while you press. Press the back crease from the hem to the crotch.

   Near the crotch area, the fabric will naturally fold, forming an "inch pinch." Press the back crease, allowing this inch pinch to form in the crotch area. Again use a Tailor Clapper® to set the crease. Allow the slacks to dry. See Fig. 7-4.

3. Insert one leg into the other, rightsides together, sewing the crotch seam and inserting a zipper if needed. (Several zipper techniques are given later in this chapter.)

### Pocket Closure

We all have clothes with zippers, buttons, button-holes, and snaps. But I like to put a closure hidden in the pocket. This technique eliminates the zipper and switches the opening to the left side pocket. For those of you not fond of setting in zippers, here's your chance to shine and to save considerable time.

This technique will only work on skirt or slacks patterns with side seam pockets and with these modifications.

1. Cut off the pocket extension from both the front and back pattern pieces and move it up to the waistline. Tape it to meet the cutting line. Note: On some patterns, the pocket extension is already positioned at the waistline. See Fig. 7-5.

2. Sew a pocket to all of the extensions, both front and back. See Fig. 7-5.

3. Sew the right side seam and pocket as the pattern guide instructs. The only change is that the pocket will be slightly higher, since the

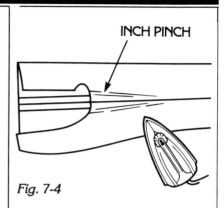

INCH PINCH

Fig. 7-4

This "inch pinch" is ambiguous, but it naturally forms in the back inner thigh. The front of the slacks remains flat. Remember to start pressing at the hem and work toward the crotch.

Fig. 7-5

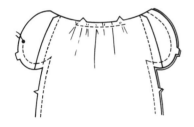

Fig. 7-6

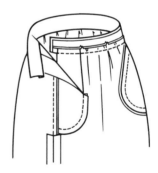

pocket extension was repositioned. See Fig. 7-6.

4. When sewing the left pocket, sew only its lower half. See Fig. 7-6.

5. Clean finish the outer edges of the left pocket with Seams Great® or by serging or zigzagging the edge.

6. Clip the back seam allowance below the pockets. Press the side seam open. Press the pockets toward the front. Machine baste the upper edges of the right pockets to the front. On the left side, machine baste only the front pocket to the skirt or slacks. See Fig. 7-7.

Your waistband will finish this closure. The waistband will begin at the left pocket opening and will extend into the pocket lining as illustrated. Be certain to cut the waistband 2-3" longer, to accommodate the waistband extension into the pocket lining.

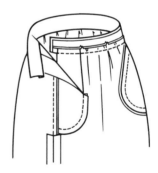

Fig. 7-7

**N N** *Later in this chapter I show you two kinds of waistbands. For this pocket closure treatment, I usually sew the fitted-looking elasticized waistband.*

## "Hand Picked" Zipper (All Done by Machine)

If I'm not sewing a pocket closure in a skirt, I usually sew in a zipper-- not an ordinary zipper, but a "hand picked" zipper. "Hand picked?" you may question. "I don't have time for that." Never fear--you can "hand pick" a zipper without leaving your sewing machine.

1. Close the zipper opening with a machine basting stitch.

2. Purchase a zipper at least 2" longer than you need. Open the zipper. Rightsides together, meet the left zipper tape to the left seam allowance, butting the zipper teeth to the basted seam. Extend the extra zipper length above the seam.

3. Machine baste the left zipper tape to the left seam allowance only. Don't sew it to the skirt itself. See Fig. 7-8.

4. Flip the zipper out so its topside is up. Fold the seam allowance away from the zipper teeth. Stitch this seam allowance 1/8" from the zipper teeth as illustrated in Fig. 7-9.

5. Close the zipper. Flip the zipper toward the right side of the garment. Fold back the skirt fabric

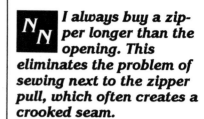

*I always buy a zipper longer than the opening. This eliminates the problem of sewing next to the zipper pull, which often creates a crooked seam.*

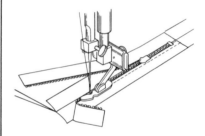

*Fig. 7-8*

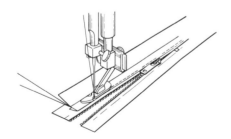

*Fig. 7-9*

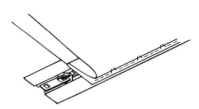

Fig. 7-10

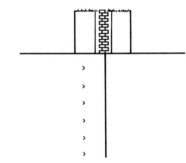

Fig. 7-12

along the right side of the zipper tape until the raw edge of the seam allowance is visible.

6. Set your machine for a blind-hem stitch and attach the blind-hem foot. Starting at the bottom of the zipper, sew with a blind-hem stitch, guiding the blind hem foot next to the garment fold. The straight stitches will go in the seam allowances, and the zag of the blind-hem stitch will catch the fold. See Figs. 7-10 and 7-11.

7. Turn the garment to the right side and remove the basting stitches. The blind-hem stitch will look like a hand picked zipper. See Fig. 7-12.

8. To trim off the excess zipper tape, *open the zipper* and bar tack across the teeth close to

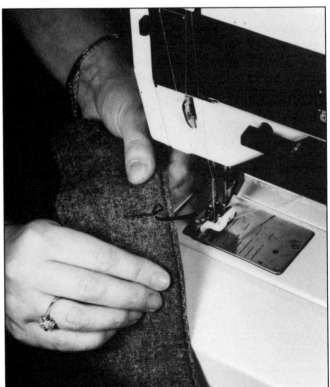

Fig. 7-11

the fabric cut edge. Cut the tape off *above* the bar tack. See Fig. 7-13.

## Two-Seam Fly Front Zipper

When you are sewing a skirt or a pair of slacks that requires a fly front zipper, here's the perfect application. Believe it or not, you can sew a fly zipper with only two rows of stitching.

1. For the standard 8" zipper opening, purchase a 9" zipper. Check the pattern to see if an adequate fly extension has been added. The extension should be 1 1/2" from the center front and should measure 9" long.

2. After cutting out the slacks, mark the center front with a nip. On the topside of the slacks, mark the center front lines with a washable marking pen. On the wrong side, mark the zipper stop point 1/2" above the bottom extension. See Fig. 7-14. If you can never remember which side is right or left, mark R and L on the topside with the washable pen.

3. Rightsides together, sew the front crotch seam, starting 1" from the inseam and ending at the dot. See Fig. 7-15. Lock your threads by changing the stitch length to 0 and stitching several times in place. (This method of locking

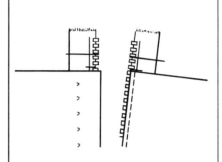

Fig. 7-13

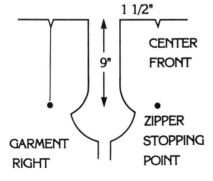

Fig. 7-14

N. N. *Zippers are usually placed in the center-front or center-back seams, not at the side seams, since our hipline curves make side-seam zippers buckle or bulge.*

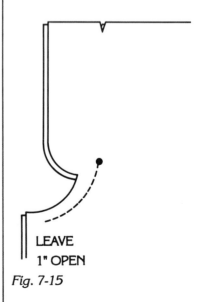

Fig. 7-15

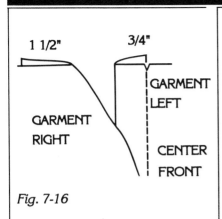

1 1/2"          3/4"

GARMENT
RIGHT

GARMENT
LEFT

CENTER
FRONT

*Fig. 7-16*

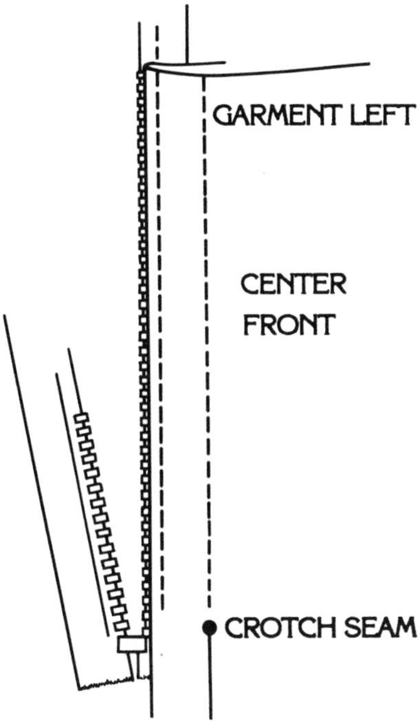

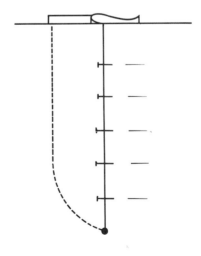

GARMENT LEFT

CENTER
FRONT

CROTCH SEAM

*Fig. 7-17*

*Always sew zippers from bottom to top. Sewing from the waistline to the bottom may create a dimple at the bottom of the zipper.*

threads is preferred over back stitching, since it doesn't create bulk or puckers.)

4. Press the left front extension under 3/4". On the right front, press the extension under 1 1/2". See Fig. 7-16.

5. Place the zipper under the left front extension. Position the bottom zipper staple directly below the zipper opening. The zipper tape will extend above the waistline. Place the fabric fold 1/8" from the zipper teeth. Stitch the fabric to the zipper tape, using a zipper foot. See Fig. 7-17.

6. Close the zipper. Lap the right front extension to the left side so the center front lines meet. Pin in place. Topstitch, beginning at the bottom of the zipper opening, and curve the stitching line to 1" from the fold. For ease of sewing, mark the stitching line with a washable marking pen. See Fig. 7-18.

7. Trim off the excess zipper tape as instructed in step 8 of hand- picked zippers.

*Fig. 7-18*

## For Skirts Only--Lining Expertise

To make a skirt hang properly and to give it a better fit, add a free- floating lining. It is not necessary to line all skirts, but this method will add body and shape to most fabrics.

This lining technique is quite different from lining instructions given on pattern guides. It requires no hand sewing and a minimum of machine sewing.

If your skirt has a hemline slit, traditional lining requires hand tacking around the slit. You will appreciate the time-saving feature of this lining. No hand sewing is necessary since the lining is curved to prevent it from peeking out of the slit.

1. Make a new pattern for the back lining. Place a length of wax paper over the pattern and with a felt-tipped pen, trace the waist, side seam, and center back cutting lines. If the center back has a pleat extension, avoid it and draw a straight cutting line as illustrated. *Trace the hemline 1/2" shorter than the finished hemline length.*

2. Note: Complete step 2 only if your skirt has a hemline slit. If it doesn't, continue with step 3. On the new pattern piece, measure up 7" from the corner of the center back at the bottom edge (A). Measure across 7" from the center back at the bottom edge (B). Measure 3" in on a diagonal line from the bottom center back (C). See Fig. 7-19. Connect the dots to form the hemline curve. Cut the back lining from this pattern shape.

3. If the front pattern piece has pockets, pin the front skirt and pocket pieces together as if they were sewn. Place wax paper over the pattern and trace around the complete skirt pattern, making the hemline 1/2" shorter than the finished length. Cut out the lining. See Fig. 7- 20.

4. Sew the front and back lining at the side seams. If the pattern has darts or pleats, only mark the

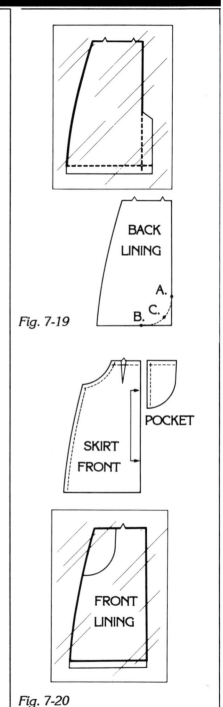

*Fig. 7-19*

*Fig. 7-20*

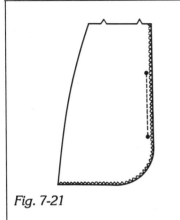

Fig. 7-21

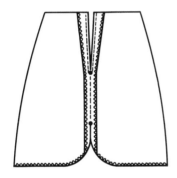

Fig. 7-22

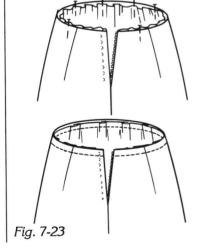

Fig. 7-23

dart placement. *Do not sew the darts or pleats.* This will be taken care of later.

5. Sew the center back seam between the zipper dot and the top of the hemline curve. See Fig. 7-21.

6. Press under 3/4" at the center back zipper opening and gradually taper to the 5/8" stitched seam allowances. Press as illustrated. This larger seam allowance will not be caught in the zipper teeth. See Fig. 7-22.

7. Since the lining is cut to the finished length, clean finish the raw edges with a zigzag stitch, Seams Great®, narrow lace, or a rolled hem on a serger.

8. Slip the lining inside the skirt with the wrong sides together. At the waistline, pin together the side seams of the outer skirt and lining. Pin the pressed-under seam allowances of the center back to the zipper area.

9. The lining will be larger than the outer skirt, since no darts or pleats have been sewn. If your skirt has darts, you will not sew them. Instead, you will take a tuck at each waistline dart position. Pin the darts and pleats to meet the contour of the skirt. (You may be taking a deeper dart tuck than normal since the lining must be smaller, in order to fit properly inside the skirt.)

10. Machine baste the skirt and lining together along the waistline. The lining's darts and pleats will look like tucks. To eliminate bulk, press the tucks in the opposite direction of the skirt dart or pleats. See Fig. 7-23.

**Belt Loops**

This easy method makes attractive, even belt loops with a minimum of bulk.

1. Cut a 1" strip of fabric on the straight of grain.

2. Thread the 1" strip through a 1/2" bias tape maker.

3. Fold the strip in half again and stitch the folded edges closed. See Fig. 7-24. Then slice into belt loops.

## Fitted-Looking Elasticized Waistband

If you like your waistband to hug your waist the way it does with an elasticized waistband, yet you also want a fitted look, use this terrific treatment. This technique can be used on any fitted skirt or slacks pattern. If you need a waistband with a lot of elasticity, alter and cut the skirt or slacks pattern and waistband 1" to 2" larger than you need. We do not interface this waistband, as it inhibits the elastic.

1. Cut a new waistband pattern 3" wide and the length of the garment's waistline plus 3" for seam allowance and underlay. Either cut the waistband along the selvage or clean finish one lengthwise seam with Seams Great®, zigzagging, or serging.

2. Pin 4" belt loops at the skirt or slacks side seams, darts, pleats, and anywhere you prefer. Raw edges of belt and waistline together, baste in place.

3. Rightsides together, pin the waistband to the garment, extending the waistband 5/8" beyond the lapped side of the zipper opening. On the underlay side, the waistband will extend 2 3/8" beyond the zipper opening. It will be finished in a later step. Sew the waistband to the waistline with a 5/8" seam. See Fig. 7-25.

4. Grade the seam allowances and press the waistband and seam allowances up.

5. At the lapped side of the zipper opening, meet the rightsides of the waistband together, extending the finished edge about 1/4" beyond the waistband seam and folding the waistband to a finished size of about 1 1/4" wide. Place

Fig. 7-24  Bias tape maker

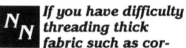 *If you have difficulty threading thick fabric such as corduroy through the bias tape maker, attach a needle and thread at one end of the strip. Drop the needle and thread through the tape maker. Pull the needle and thread to advance the fabric.*

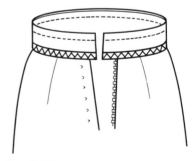

Fig. 7-25

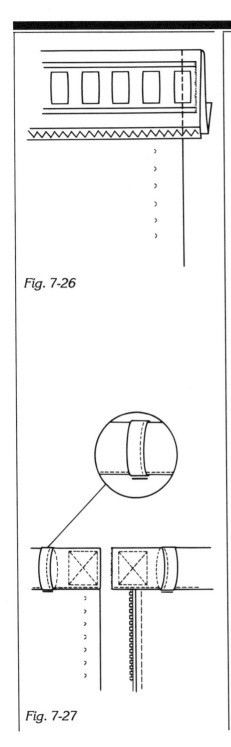

Fig. 7-26

Fig. 7-27

3/4" or 1" non-roll elastic on top of the waistband. Cut the elastic slightly longer than the waistband. (Later, you'll learn how to cut the elastic to size.) See Fig. 7-26.

6. Sew the waistline center back seam, including the elastic in the seam allowances. Stitch a second time. Grade seam allowances and angle cut the corner. Before turning the waistband rightside out, place a safety pin or elastic glide, a notion which guides elastic through a casing, preventing the elastic from twisting, at the end of the elastic. See Fig. 7-27.

7. Turn the waistband rightside out and press to the finished size.

8. Working from the garment's topside, stitch-in-the-ditch in the waistline seam. This stitching will attach the underside of the waistband. The elastic, however, will still be floating inside the waistband. See Fig. 7-27.

9. Try on your garment and pull the elastic to the correct tightness. Put a safety pin through the underlay and elastic, to hold it in place. Then cut off the excess elastic. If you are inserting this elastic in a traditional fitted waistband, you will only cut about 1" from the elastic. If you are inserting it into a waistband that you cut 1" to 2" larger, you will cut off several inches of elastic.

10. Finish the waistband by zigzagging the unfinished end of the waistband, sewing through all the layers. (If you prefer, sewing with a satin stitch, rather than an open zigzag, will give a finished look to this raw edge.) The elastic will be caught in this sewing. Trim off any excess elastic or fabric whiskers. See Fig. 7-27. Attach the free ends of the belt loops by folding them over the waistband to the underside and stitching with a bar tack in the ditch. Sew a decorative box on both the lapped and underneath sides of the waistband, to keep the elastic flat at the closure. If you want to

hide the box on the topside, sew a button over it.

## Contoured Waistband

Most fitted waistband pattern pieces are drafted the length of the waistline with added extensions for the closure. The grainline follows the length of the waistband, giving stability. If you have a slight swayback, however, this waistband will stand away from your body. In order to make the waistband hug your waistline, draft a contoured waistband.

The contoured waistband hugs your back, because the back of the waistband is bias cut and the side seam allowances are angled to give the band a contoured shape. Any waistband pattern can be changed to this style.

1. The standard waistband pattern is marked with two vertical dots (:) or a square ( ■ ), indicating the side seams. Place a length of wax paper over the front section of the waistband. Trace the front section to the side seam markings. See Fig. 7-28.

2. Instead of cutting a one-piece waistband that is folded over at the top of the waistband, the contoured waistband will be seamed at the top. Therefore, you need to add a 5/8" seam allowance. On the wax paper, make the top stitching line fall on the fold of the original pattern. Then add 5/8" seam allowances to the fold and side seam. Mark the original grainline on the new front pattern. Write "Cut 4" on the pattern. See Fig. 7-29.

 *I belong to a sewing group that meets every Tuesday morning. In this group we share the latest techniques that someone read about, what new fabric line the local store received, what's in the mail-order catalogs, etc. This is a real time-saver for me. I do not have time to read all the magazines I want, to visit the stores on a weekly basis, and so forth.*

**Cindi Baker**
**Cary, NC**

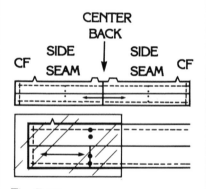

Fig. 7-28

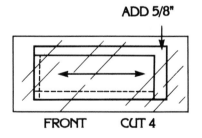

Fig. 7-29

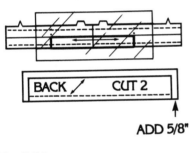

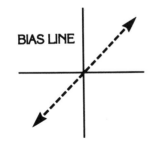

ADD 5/8"

Fig. 7-30

BIAS LINE

Fig. 7-31

3. Trace a new back pattern between the sets of vertical dots or squares. Add a 5/8" seam allowance on each side. Again, mark a stitching line at the fold of the traditional waistband and add a 5/8" seam allowance. See Fig. 7-30. Mark the center back with a vertical line and intersect it with the original pattern's grainline drawn for 2" on either side of the center back.

4. Add a bias grainline on the back waistband by folding a diagonal at the center back. See Fig. 7-31. The center back line should meet the right grain line. Open up the pattern and draw a new bias grainline on the folded diagonal. Mark it "Grainline" and add arrows so you won't get confused about grainlines when you're cutting out. Write "Cut 2" on the new back pattern.

5. For additional contouring of the back waistband, measure in 1/2" on the top of each side of the back waistband. Draw new cutting lines. See Fig. 7-32.

6. Interface all waistband pieces with fusible interfacing the same weight as your fashion fabric. Don't use an interfacing that's too crisp. Cut the interfacing pattern minus a 1/2" seam allowance. Cut the interfacing following the same grainlines you marked for the fashion

1/2" _____ 1/2"

Fig. 7-32

fabric. (If your interfacing is considered "all-bias," you may ignore the grainlines on the interfacing pattern pieces and cut in any direction.) Fuse to waistband pieces.

7. Sew the waistband together at the side seams. See Fig. 7-33.

8. Rightsides together, sew the inner and outer waistbands along the upper edge. Grade the seam allowances and understitch. I like to use a multiple zigzag or serpentine stitch, for added stability at the upper edge.

9. Attach the waistband to the waistline of the slacks or skirt, following the directions on the pattern guide.

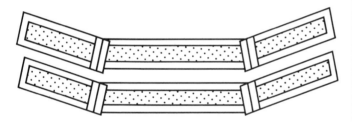

Fig. 7-33

*I waste a lot of time trying to thread a sewing-machine needle (young spirit, old eyes). Then I found that when I bent my wire needle threader in a right angle, I could easily insert it from the back of the needle, thread it, and pull it through.*

**Roberta Patterson**
**West Lafayette, IN**

*How do I find time to sew? Easy-- retire.*

**Arlene Ray**
**Blythe, CA**

# CHAPTER 8

# LINGERIE: TIME-AFFORDABLE SEWING

 *How do I find time for sewing? Simple-- go shopping for ready-to-wear! When I find myself with "no time to sew," only time to shop, then off I go. After driving to the mall, cruising to find a parking space, walking to the store, up the escalator, rummaging through the racks, waiting in line to try on the clothes, I often end up not buying, even if the clothes fit. I can't stand the poor workmanship, inferior and dirty fabrics, missing buttons, etc. If I do buy, I have to wait in another line to pay.*

*Add up all the time involved with just one store, let alone more, and I run back to my machine and catalogs to put the same amount of time into making a much better all-around garment.*

*Kathleen Cullen*
*Island Park, NY*

Sewing lingerie is surprisingly time-affordable, since you can sew a half- slip and camisole in an hour, or five pairs of undies in an evening. The money saved is also attractive, but my greatest enjoyment in sewing lingerie is finishing so many garments in such a short time.

If you have never worked with nylon tricot, lingerie fabric, read the following discussion of fabric and notions. They will cut your sewing time and make lingerie sewing possible for even the busiest woman. I will then show you how to make some half-slip variations, for quick practice on sewing with tricot. Patterns for camisoles, underpants, and other lingerie are readily available in fabric stores or you can consult the mail-order section at the end of the book.

### Lingerie Fabric and Notion Selections

**Non-cling tricot**, such as Antron III, has an obvious advantage over the standard tricot. It costs about $1.50/yard more than the traditional clinging type, but its non-cling characteristic is well worth the price.

Many of us use washable marking pens with blue ink for garment sewing. They are extremely helpful when quartering lingerie elastic, for example. Since lingerie sewing is so fast, you can also use a **vanishing marking pen** with purple ink (generally used for quilting) that disappears within 48 hours. The marks will disappear after you finish sewing.

The most important notion for lingerie sewing is the needle. When lingerie sewing first became popular, the suggested needle was a ball-point or Yellow Band needle. These needles are still useful, but the new **stretch needle** is especially designed for tricot and delicate knits. The rounded point allows the needle to slip between the fibers without catching or snagging.

If you plan to sew a lot of lingerie, consider investing in **super fine pins.** These pins are long and extremely fine. They are designed for silks, silky-polys, and nylon tricot.

A **washable fabric glue stick** is extremely handy when applying lingerie lace. A little bit of this glue goes a long way.

The basic lingerie sewing supplies have not changed over the years. When looking for these basics--**lace, elastic, and thread**--remember to look for a polyester or nylon fiber content and buy 100% polyester or core-spun polyester thread. These notions will then have the same properties as the tricot.

## Lingerie Basics

### Cutting

When cutting tricot, keep in mind that the greatest amount of stretch (crossgrain) must go around your figure.

To find the right side of the tricot, pull the fabric horizontally on the crossgrain. It will curl or roll to the right side. Mark the right side with a washable pen or with a piece of tape.

### Patterns

Many half-slip patterns are multi-sized. Instead of cutting your master pattern apart, use Trace-A-Pattern® or wax paper to trace off your slip size.

Since one width of wax paper may not be wide enough for your lingerie pattern, fuse two lengths of paper together with a warm iron. The wax will not hurt your iron, but if you don't like the idea, cover your sole plate with aluminum foil and let it heat up.

### Seams

Keep in mind these two general rules when sewing seams in lingerie:

**1. Hold both threads and start sewing 1/4" from the end.**

This prevents the fabric from being pulled down into the opening in the throat plate. You can also use an anchor cloth, as shown in Chapter 3.

 *A great many of us cannot close a door and leave our sewing to be picked up later exactly where we left it. Since putting away sewing and getting it out again is so time- consuming, cutting down on this part gives us more time for actual sewing. Here is where a bit of planning will help.*

*Before starting a project, gather everything that will be needed to finish the project and find a box that will hold everything. A flat box like a suit box works fine. As you sew, put everything back into the box. Lay the last piece you were working on at the top of the pile. It helps you remember exactly at what point you had to stop. The box saves a lot of time in cleaning up and getting things out again. It also helps keep things smooth and in good condition.*

*Amy Jane Raffety
Sierra Vista, AZ*

*Fig. 8-2*

*For lingerie method 2B, I use the ability to mirror a stitch on my computer machine to stitch the blind-hem, so that the bulk of the fabric is still to the left of the machine.*

*Robbie*

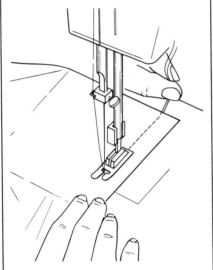

Fig. 8-1

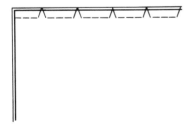

Fig. 8-3

### 2. As you sew, stretch the fabric slightly both in front and in back of the presser foot.

This stops the seam from puckering. See Fig. 8-1. Decide which of the following seam constructions you want to use:

### A. Two Rows of Zigzag

Use the standard 1/4" seam allowances. Sew with a narrow width and a short stitch length. The first row of zigzag should be on the 1/4" seam and the second row on the 1/8" seam. See Fig. 8-2.

### B. Blind-Hem Stitch (Fig. 8-3)

Used unconventionally, this is a wonderful stitch for tricot. It both creates the seam and overlocks the edge, but you must sew with the bulk of the fabric to the right of the presser foot. See Fig. 8-4. Experiment on a scrap to find out where to guide the presser foot. The zag of the blind-hem stitch should fall off the fabric.

Fig. 8-4

### C. Serged Seam

Use a 3- or 3/4-thread serger to sew lingerie. Test on a scrap of fabric to find the correct stitch length and width for your tricot. Each looper thread should lie smooth and flat. See Fig. 8-5.

### Lace Application

Many hemlines of half-slips and camisoles are completely edged with lace. Here are some tips on applying lace.

- Lap the straight edge of the lace on top of the right side of the tricot.

- Before sewing a section of lace to the tricot, finger baste the two layers together, gently holding the layers together, and then sew the section. Finger basting will prevent the lace from stretching. See Fig. 8-6. You can also use a washable fabric glue stick to hold the lace in place.

*I like to use woolly nylon thread on the loopers of my serger when serging lingerie. This thread is not twisted like regular thread. It is texturized, producing a softer, more comfortable seam.*

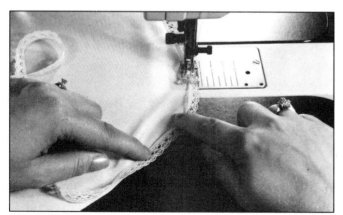
*Fig. 8-6*

*Fig. 8-5*

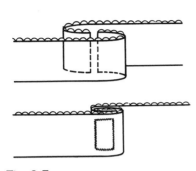

Fig. 8-7

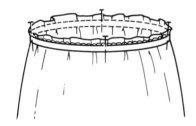

Fig. 8-8

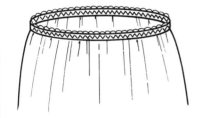

Fig. 8-9

- Attach the lace by using a tiny zigzag stitch (e.g., stitch width 1 and stitch length 1 or 18 stitches/inch).

### Elastics

Many instructions ask us to cut the elastic 2-3" smaller than our waistlines. Since all elastics are not created equal--they may be knitted, woven, braided and made of many different fiber contents--they behave differently. Thus, this flat-sizing guide is not 100% accurate.

Instead, I like to size and sew elastic with this easy common-sense approach.

### One-Step Method

1. Measure the elastic by placing it around your waist so it fits comfortably. Check to see if this length will stretch over your hips. Cut.

2. Join the elastic ends to form a ring, overlapping 1/2". Turn both raw edges under and stitch a rectangle using a tiny zigzag stitch. See Fig. 8-7.

3. Divide the elastic and the waistline of the slip into four equal parts. Mark each quarter with a washable marking pen.

4. Place the scalloped edge of the elastic about 1" down from the top edge of the topside of the slip, matching the quartering marks. Pin the elastic to the slip at each mark. See Fig. 8-8.

5. Using a zigzag or multiple zigzag stitch, set your machine at its widest width and a 1 length (18 stitches/inch). Sew along the lower edge of the elastic, stretching it to meet the fabric. After sewing, trim away the excess tricot at the top of the elastic. Since tricot does not ravel, this will be a clean finish. See Fig. 8-9.

### Two-Step Method

The next technique gives a neater finish, but takes two sewing steps. Since the elastic will be sewn twice, which increases the chances of the elastic losing its stretch, check this first on a sample. You *must* use a stretch needle for this application, since this needle does not pierce the elastic.

1. Follow steps 1-3 for the One-Step Method (Figs. 8-7 to 8-9).
2. On the right side of the tricot, place the straight edge of the elastic next to the raw edge of the waistline. Match the quarter marks of the elastic to the quarter marks of the waistline. Pin in place. See Fig. 8-10.
3. Using a medium width zigzag (2) and a medium length stitch (2), sew along the scalloped edge of the elastic. Stretch the elastic to meet the fabric. See Fig. 8-11.
4. Turn the elastic to the wrong side. The scalloped edge of the elastic will now be on top. Stitch with a straight or zigzag stitch near the bottom edge of the elastic, stretching the fabric flat. See Fig. 8-12.

## The Busy Woman's Half-Slip

You will need:

- 3/4 yard of nylon tricot
- 3/4 yard of 1/2" lace
- 3/4 yard of lingerie elastic

1. To make a pattern, cut a rectangle of tricot your hip measurement plus 4" and 27" long (or any length you prefer). Make sure the stretch of the fabric goes around your hips. See Fig. 8-13.

Fig. 8-10

Fig. 8-11

Fig. 8-12

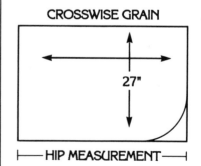

CROSSWISE GRAIN

27"

HIP MEASUREMENT

Fig. 8-13    PLUS 4"

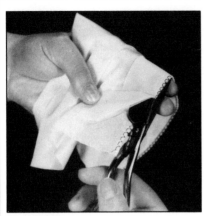

Fig. 8-14

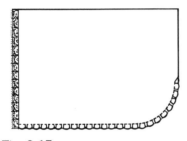

Fig. 8-15

 *Trimming close to stitching is done easiest by beveling the scissors. To bevel, place your scissors on the same level as the fabric, to allow the blade of the scissors to lie extremely close to the stitching. Cut carefully. I like to use applique scissors for this step. Their bill protects the main fabric from being cut.*

2. With the topside of the fabric facing you, trim the lower right-hand corner into a slight curve. See Fig. 8-13.

3. Scallop the lower edge and curved end by using the blind-hem stitch. First, fold under 1/2" of the tricot. On the topside, sew over the folded edge by sewing with the bulk of the fabric to the right of the presser foot (see Fig. 8-4). End the scallop about 1/2" from the top of the curved area (see Fig. 8-15). Trim away the excess tricot from the scalloped edge. See Fig. 8-14. The left straight edge is not scalloped.

4. Apply lace to the straight edge of the slip (see Fig. 8-6). At the hem edge, turn under the lace to clean finish it. See Fig. 8-15.

5. Overlap the laced edge of the slip 1/2" on top of the unfinished side. With glue stick, baste the two layers together.

6. Stitch the two layers together with a zigzag stitch on the overlapped area. Apply the elastic according to one of the two methods described earlier. See Fig. 8-16.

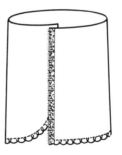 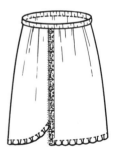

Fig. 8-16

*To evenly distribute the glue-basting, glide a warm iron over the basted area. You'll be surprised at the even, temporary bond this will give.*

## Creative Sewing With Half-Slips

Because half-slips are so fast to make, you can easily add decorative accents to personalize them. They make wonderful gifts and only you know how little they cost in time and money.

### *Decorative Stitches*

I do not always use the decorative stitches or cams on my sewing machine to their fullest potential. Here are some ideas on how to use them on lingerie.

Instead of sewing lace to the hemline, use decorative stitches.

1. Cut the half-slip 2 1/2" longer than needed. Gently press up the hem.

2. To prevent the tricot from stretching, place a layer of supportive fabric like Tear Away®, water-soluble stabilizer, or paper under the pressed hem.

3. From the right side, stitch multiple rows of decorative stitches. After sewing, remove the supportive paper or fabric under the pressed hem. See Fig. 8-17.

### *Lace Insertion*

A perfect gift idea is to give a slip that can be shortened. Here's how:

1. Sew the first row of lace to the very edge of the hemline.

2. Use a glue stick to baste additional rows of lace at the bottom of the slip, making the rows 2-3" apart. Zigzag or serge along each side of the lace. See Fig. 8-18.

*Fig. 8-17*

*Fig. 8-18*

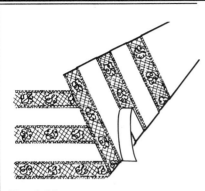

Fig. 8-19

Fig. 8-20

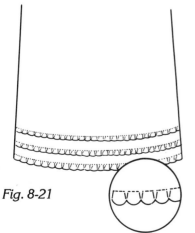

Fig. 8-21

3. Trim away the tricot from behind the lace, close to the stitching. (Applique scissors make this an easy task.) See Fig. 8-19.

Now the slip can be shortened by cutting off a section immediately below the lace. The edge is still nicely finished with lace. See Fig. 8-20.

### Shell Edging

Once again, we will use the versatile blind-hem stitch (and you thought it was only for hemming!).

1. Cut the hemline 2-3" longer than needed. Gently press up the hem.

2. Set your machine for a blind-hem stitch, widest width (4) and short length (1). Stitch along the fold, sewing with the greatest amount of fabric to the right of the presser foot, as you did in Fig. 8-4.

3. Make several rows of shell edging by folding the fabric every 1" from the previous row and repeating step 2. See Fig. 8-21.

As an alternate trim, use a 3- or 3/4-thread serger and sew rows of overlocking along the edges.

In fact, lingerie is a good place to practice decorative serging techniques like flatlocking, rolled edging, French hand sewing, and more. My favorite book on these techniques is **Creative Serging Illustrated** by Pati Palmer, Gail Brown, and Sue Green (see Resource section at end of book.)

*When I have perfected a pattern and am ready to use it over and over, I like to put clear Contact paper on the back of the pattern pieces. (It also discourages me from gaining weight!)*

# A Final Word

*I hope that you have enjoyed reading and working with this book as much as I have enjoyed sharing my techniques with you.*

*I'd like to remind you of two last things. While it's wonderful to have a wardrobe that's fashionable, comfortable, and hand-crafted, the wardrobe is merely the end result. It's the process of sewing that's such a pleasure--handling fabric, revelling in color and texture, maneuvering a fine tool like the sewing machine or serger, building something out of nothing. Make the process of sewing a pleasure for yourself, so that you hum and smile to yourself as you sew.*

*And secondly, consider spreading the joy to others. With sewing no longer taught in many schools, those of us blessed with a love of sewing must volunteer on our own. If nothing else, take your machine to a local nursery school and let the children see you sew. Better yet, teach your children (both sexes) and your neighbors' children (and your grown-up neighbors too!) how to sew simple things like napkins and tablecloths, pillows, T- shirts, gathered shorts, and such.*

*But no matter how busy you are, after a day of shopping, cooking, cleaning, sewing, working, planning, and child rearing, be sure to make time to relax. As my Grandpa Larson always urged me to do, "Smell the roses of life."*

# Profile of a Busy Woman
### by Robbie Fanning

With a successful mail-order business employing 38 people, a weekly TV show, extensive writing and lecturing commitments, and a family, Nancy Zieman is one busy woman. Yet she still sews most of her wardrobe and makes gifts for family and friends. How does she find time to sew?

"For me," she replies, "sewing is more than a job. I started sewing when I was 10 and I still love it, so it's not hard for me to find time here and there for something that gives me so much pleasure."

A typical day for Nancy begins about 6 a.m., when she cleans up and does laundry until her family rises. Husband Rich and Nancy breakfast with four-year-old Ted and then go to work together at the Nancy's Notion warehouse in Beaver Dam, WS. Rich supervises the mail-order business, while Nancy plans the TV shows and the notions which will be included in the catalog.

Nancy has a personal staff of three to help her with the tremendous planning, sewing, and paperwork that go into the business and the TV show. For example, they spent about 150 hours preparing the "Knit, Serge and Sew" videotape.

At noon she and Rich go home to lunch with Ted and his babysitter. Then they return to the warehouse and work until 5 p.m.

Nancy fixes dinner and the family then participates in community affairs. Rich is enrolled in the Bethel Bible Study series and sings in the church choir. Nancy teaches Sunday School at Peace Lutheran Church and is on the boards of the local United Way and of the Beaver Dam Community Hospital. Both Rich and Nancy also have many relatives in the area.

Later at night, Nancy goes into her sewing room and sews until she gets tired. "It's funny that I am in the sewing business all day and then sew at night, but I find it very soothing after a long day at work."

This routine is altered periodically by trips to Madison to tape her weekly TV show, "Sewing With Nancy," shown on two cable-TV channels (The Learning Channel and Tempo) and on Public Television Stations. She also lectures nationally and travels to trade shows.

All of this has grown from a simple seed: Nancy's love of sewing. Nancy's mother, Barbara Luedtke, of Larsen, WS, helped nuture the seed. "I was a 4-H leader for 24 years," she says. "Nancy started sewing for 4-H when she was 10 and I can still see that first gathered skirt she made. 4-H was good training, because you have to keep track of what you do--put little swatches of fabric on cards and document everything. By her third year, Nancy made a shirtwaist. She always did a good job and loved sewing.

"Our cash flow wasn't too great, with four kids and a dairy farm. But sewing helped us stretch our dollars. Nancy and I worked together all through high school to get more clothes for less money."

When Nancy had been 18 months old, an earache had caused a nerve to swell, which in turn caused a condition called Bell's palsy. The nerve died, restricting mobility in Nancy's face. "They say Mona Lisa's mysterious smile is because she had Bell's palsy," says Nancy. "Coping with my condition as I grew up was sometimes difficult. But my success at sewing was like therapy for me and by the time I was a freshman in high school, I knew I wanted to do something with sewing as a career."

Nancy majored in clothing and textiles at the University of Wisconsin- Stout. Her first job out of college was as home economist for a Minnesota Fabrics store in Chicago. Rich Zieman, with a college background in business and economics, was manager of the store. Before long, the two married. Nancy then worked for the SewFit Company, co-authoring a book on fit.

In 1979, Rich, now working for a furniture company, was transferred to a small town in northern Minnesota. Nancy had no employment opportunities there, so she began free-lance lecturing about new sewing techniques. As a part of her lectures, she demonstrated the latest tools and notions. People in the audience always asked where they could get the tools, so on October 1, 1979, Nancy's Notions was founded, with an 8 1/2 x 11 flyer.

By 1981 Nancy opened her first warehouse and in 1983, Rich joined her full-time in the business. In the meantime Nancy had tired of travelling to lecture so much, especially with a new baby. In 1983, an opportunity arose to film a cable-TV show on sewing. Nancy realized she could now communicate her love of sewing to a wide audience without the strenuous travel. "Sewing With Nancy" has appeared on two cable-TV stations for 4 1/2 years and in 1987, was picked up for distribution on Public Television Stations.

Today, Nancy is as busy as any woman who works full-time and has a family, yet she still manages to sneak in a few hours a day for what she loves: sewing.

# Glossary

**anchor cloth**
a pad of scrap fabric sewn over before sewing the fashion fabric and later cut off; prevents snarling stitches at the beginning of a line of stitching

**bevel**
to hold scissors at a 45 degree angle to the seam allowance; causes automatic grading of the seams

**chain stitching**
sewing or serging together garment pieces, one after the other, without clipping threads between pieces until all sewing is finished

**crosswise grain**
an imaginary line perpendicular to the selvage

**directional sewing**
stitching from the widest part to the narrowest (e.g., from the bottom of a skirt to the waist)

**fabric hand**
the feeling of fabric as you grasp it in your hand (e.g., soft hand, crisp hand)

**finger easing**
placing the right or left finger behind the presser foot and slowing the flow of fabric under the foot, resulting in an eased or gathered fabric

**finger pinning**
using your fingers as if they were pins, to hold fabric layers together

**fringe foot**
(also called tailor-tacking foot) a presser foot with a raised bar on it that causes a wider, looser satin stitch which can be cut into fringe or tailor tacks

*My two main hobbies are reading and sewing. I found that I really had a hard time finding time for both. One day while at the local library, I found that they had a great number of books on cassettes, so now I can sew up a storm and still hear a book.*

*Eleanor S. Bowlus*
*Fredericktown, OH*

*From years of questioning other women, I know that you need a definite place to sew, someplace where the machine can be left open and the work spread out. When the children were small, I had a built-in desk nook in the basement rec room. Now I have converted the small spare bedroom. The machine is always open and I find an hour of sewing in the evening before bed to be very relaxing.*

*Mary Jo Kush*
*Detroit, MI*

*I always have more than one project going at a time. I store each project in a separate plastic sweater box. That way I can see which is which. The plastic box makes it portable, so I can take it with me whenever I have some free time to sew (e.g., watching TV with the family). I also keep my most used notions (scissors, seam gauge, thimble, pins, needles, beeswax, etc.) in a Rubbermaid® Roughneck carry caddy. I leave it on my sewing table, so I always know where to find my notions. They don't get knocked off the table while sewing or wrapped in my sewing project and put away. I can easily take the caddy with me. I also always read the entire pattern instructions sheet before I sew and pin together all the pieces as far as possible before I begin to sew. This is portable work and saves a lot of time at the sewing machine.*

*Mrs. Richard Farrar*
*St. Charles, MO*

**grading**
the practice of reducing bulk in enclosed seam allowances such as collars; each layer is cut closer to the seam line, the seam allowance nearest the outside of the garment being cut the longest

**grainline**
any imaginary line on the fabric running parallel to the selvages

**grainline pin**
one of a line of pins running parallel to the grainline

**lock stitch**
two or three stitches in one place to lock threads

**nips**
1/4" scissor clips into a seam allowance to mark a notch, dart, tuck, fold line, or other important point on the fabric

**placket**
a neck or sleeve opening

**selvage**
literally, "self edge"; the long edges of fabric that do not ravel because the crosswise yarns (weft) wrap around the lengthwise yarns (warp)

**shade off**
the shadow cast by fusible interfacing on the fashion fabric, causing the latter to look darker where it was fused

**shape pressing**
pressing a garment over a rounded surface like a tailor's ham to preserve a curve (e.g., a dart)

**sleeve head**
a long narrow rectangle of fleece sewn into the sleeve cap to hold it erect

## stitching-in-the-ditch

stitching from the topside exactly where two seam allowances have been seamed--i.e., in the "ditch"

## supportive fabric

anything used under the fashion fabric to give it extra support--most commonly, tear-away stabilizer, paper (typing or wax), interfacing, or water-soluble stabilizer

## tear-away

a non-woven interfacing designed to tear easily from stitching

## tricot

(pronounced tree'-ko) a finely knit wide nylon fabric used for lingerie

## understitching

pressing seam allowances toward a facing and stitching on the facing close to the seam, in order to prevent the facing from rolling to the topside

## water-soluble stabilizer

a sheet of plastic fabric that dissolves when wetted

## wrapped corner

instead of stitching a continuous 90 degree angle at a corner, two lines are stitched, the seam allowances of the second line wrapping toward the undercollar (see Fig. 4-22)

Note: I hope I have defined all the terms new to you. If you are still unsure of any other term used in this book, write me c/o of Open Chain Publishing, PO Box 2634-B, Menlo Park, CA 94026. I'll define your term in a future edition of this book.

 *First and most important, I find time because I love sewing. I sew all my own clothes plus sew for my two daughters, daughter-in-law, and alterations for my mother-in-law who is in a nursing home. One thing that really simplified my life was having my colors done at Fashion Academy. We're all Autumns, so my cupboards are stocked only with autumn colors.*

*Ruth Beamish*
*Newport Beach, CA*

 *During my working days, I would sew each night. This was the greatest therapy for me, really relaxed those tight nerves. Today, I purchase fabric, sew it up, and when the time is right, I see to it that the "Kings Aid Group" gets these items and they deliver them to the needy anywhere in the United States. It is great to help others. After all, just how many new clothes do I need?*

*Laurine Christ*
*Wells, MN*

# Notes

# Resources: Keeping up to Date

## Books and Videos--Recent Favorites

(Note: My bookshelves are full of good sewing books, too many to list here. Be sure to check your local public library in the 646.4 section.)

**Busy Woman's Sewing Techniques I and II** (two-hour video), Nancy Zieman, Nancy's Notions, 1987

**The Complete Book of Machine Embroidery**, Robbie and Tony Fanning, Chilton Book Co, 1986

**Creative Serging Illustrated**, Pati Palmer, Gail Brown, and Sue Green, Chilton Book Co, 1987

**Know Your Sewing Machine**, Jackie Dodson, Chilton Book Co, 1988

**Power Sewing/Designer Details Made Easy** (two-hour video), Sandra Betzina, Power Sewing, 1987.

## Mail-Order Companies

(Note: Watch the ads in the sewing magazines for more companies.)

**Britex-by-Mail**
146 Geary St
San Francisco, CA 94108

**Fabrics by Lineweaver**
3300 Battleground Ave
Greensboro, NC 27410

**G Street Fabrics**
11854 Rockville Pl
Rockville, MD 20852

**Keiffers** (lingerie fabric)
1625 Hennepin Ave
Minneapolis, MN 55403

**Nancy's Notions**
PO Box 683-BK
Beaver Dam, WI 53916

## Sewing Magazines and Newsletters

(Note: The major pattern companies-- Butterick, McCall, Simplicity, Vogue--all have magazines, available at fabric stores)

**Sensational Stitches Newsletter**
PO Box 1936
Orem, UT 84057

**Sew It Seams**
PO Box 2698
Kirkland, WA 98083

**Sew News**
PO Box 1790
Peoria, IL 61656

**The Sewing Sampler Newsletter**
PO Box 39
Springfield, MN 56087

**Sewing Update Newsletter**
**Serger Update Newsletter**
2269 Chestnut #269
San Francisco, CA 94123

**The Silver Thimble Newsletter**
311 Valley Brook Rd
McMurray, PA 15317

## Groups

**American Sewing Guild**
PO Box 50936
Indianapolis, IN 46250
(groups in all major cities)

# Family Measurements

*(write in pencil)*

| Name | | | | Standard Ease |
|------|------|------|------|------|
| Date | | | | |
| Bust or Chest | | | | 3-4" |
| Waist | | | | 1" |
| Hips | | | | 2" (slacks) |
| | | | | 4" (skirts) |
| Arm Length | | | | |

Other:

| | | | | |
|------|------|------|------|------|
| | | | | |
| | | | | |
| | | | | |
| | | | | |
| | | | | |
| | | | | |
| | | | | |

# THE BUSY WOMAN'S SEWING RECORD

| Date (Season and Year) | | | | |
|---|---|---|---|---|
| **Blazer Pattern (Company, #)** | | | | |
| Cost: | | | | |
| Fabric: | | | | |
| Fabric Cost: | | | | |
| Interfacing: | | | | |
| Interfacing Cost: | | | | |
| Notions: | | | | |
| Notions Cost: | | | | |
| Total Approximate Cost: | | | | |
| **Blouse Pattern:** | | | | |
| Cost: | | | | |
| Fabric: | | | | |
| Fabric Cost: | | | | |
| Interfacing: | | | | |
| Interfacing Cost: | | | | |
| Notions: | | | | |
| Notions Cost: | | | | |
| Total Approximate Cost: | | | | |
| **Dress Pattern:** | | | | |
| Cost: | | | | |
| Fabric: | | | | |
| Fabric Cost: | | | | |
| Interfacing: | | | | |
| Interfacing Cost: | | | | |
| Notions: | | | | |
| Notions Cost: | | | | |
| Total Approximate Cost: | | | | |

| Date (Season and Year) | | | | |
|---|---|---|---|---|
| **Skirt Pattern:** | | | | |
| Cost: | | | | |
| Fabric: | | | | |
| Fabric Cost: | | | | |
| Interfacing: | | | | |
| Interfacing Cost: | | | | |
| Notions: | | | | |
| Notions Cost: | | | | |
| Total Approximate Cost: | | | | |
| **Slacks Pattern:** | | | | |
| Cost: | | | | |
| Fabric: | | | | |
| Fabric Cost: | | | | |
| Interfacing: | | | | |
| Interfacing Cost: | | | | |
| Notions: | | | | |
| Notions Cost: | | | | |
| Total Approximate Cost: | | | | |
| **Lingerie:** | | | | |
| Cost: | | | | |
| Fabric: | | | | |
| Fabric Cost: | | | | |
| Interfacing: | | | | |
| Interfacing Cost: | | | | |
| Notions: | | | | |
| Notions Cost: | | | | |
| Total Approximate Cost: | | | | |

# Index

# Invitations

 We appreciate your feedback on this book. Other readers have helped us correct typos and clear up misunderstandings. Feel free to write me at:

**Nancy's Notions**
**PO Box 683-BK5**
**Beaver Dam, WI 53916**

Sorry--letters cannot be individually answered.

Also available from Nancy's Notions:

**The Busy Woman's Fitting Book**
**The Slacks Fitting Book (pattern included)**

*For your free catalog of books, notions, and fabrics, send to the address above.*

If your area Public Television does not carry "Sewing With Nancy" and you would like to see the show, contact the Program Director at the station (look in the Yellow Pages under Television Stations) and tell him or her it is available through Central Educational Network, Des Plaines, IL.

 Do you have a time-saving tip to share for future editions of this book? Send it to me at Nancy's Notions.